MAKING LIFE MAKE SENSE

Campus Life Books

After You Graduate
Against All Odds: True Stories of People Who Never Gave Up
Alive: Daily Devotions
Alive 2: Daily Devotions
The Campus Life Guide to Dating
The Campus Life Guide to Making and Keeping Friends
The Campus Life Guide to Surviving High School
Do You Sometimes Feel Like a Nobody?
Life at McPherson High
The Life of the Party: A True Story of Teenage Alcoholism
The Lighter Side of Campus Life
A Love Story: Questions and Answers on Sex
Making Life Make Sense
Peer Pressure: Making It Work for You
Personal Best: A Campus Life Guide to Knowing and Liking Yourself
Welcome to High School
What Teenagers Are Saying about Drugs and Alcohol
Worth the Wait: Love, Sex, and Keeping the Dream Alive
You Call This a Family? Making Yours Better

Answers to Hard Questions About God & You

JAY KESLER WITH TIM STAFFORD

Making Life Make Sense

Published by Zondervan Publishing House
1415 Lake Drive S.E., Grand Rapids, Michigan 49506

Library of Congress Cataloging-in-Publication Data

Kesler, Jay.
[Breakthrough]
Making life make sense / Jay Kesler with Tim Stafford.
p. cm.
Originally published under title: Breakthrough.
Summary: Examines many questions young people may have about God and Christianity.
ISBN 0-310-71191-6
1. God—Juvenile literature. 2. Youth—Religious life. 3. Christian life—1960- —Juvenile literature. [1. God. 2. Christian life.] I. Stafford, Tim. II. Title.
BT107.K47 1991
231—dc20 90-23130
CIP
AC

Printed in the United States of America

91 92 93 94 95 96 / CH / 10 9 8 7 6 5 4 3 2 1

To the staff men and women of Youth for Christ
who give their lives to introduce
young people to the Savior, and
who live their lives incarnationally
before them.

Contents

Preface

Each chapter in this book asks and wrestles with a major question of faith—a question about knowing God or about living with him. These questions are ones I've had to struggle with—barriers I think we all have to break through if we're going to have a vital faith, a meaningful relationship with God.

At the end of each chapter is a short section designed to help you take off in your own thinking. You'll be asked to react directly to some of the ideas presented in the chapter. Sometimes further questions are suggested for you to think about. I've also included additional Scripture I think will spur your thinking. Plus you'll find a list of books I've found helpful in tackling each question covered here.

You could use the "takeoffs" as a solitary exercise for your own personal growth. Or, if you're reading this book with a friend or as part of a group study, the "takeoffs" could serve as interaction starters for discussing what you read.

I'd rather you didn't just swallow everything I say as you read this book. What you believe will mean a lot more to you if you struggle with your own questions and dig for answers you can base your life on.

A major portion of this book first appeared in my regular *Campus Life* Magazine column and in two earlier books I wrote with Tim Stafford: *I Never Promised You a Disneyland* and *Outside Disneyland.* That material has been restructured here. As you read about the questions I've asked, I hope you find answers to yours.

—Jay Kesler

Part I

UNDERSTANDING GOD

Part I

Understanding God

Walking down the steps of that inner-city church, I felt the tired relief of knowing my speaking engagement was over and I'd soon be on my way home. But before I reached my car I heard a voice calling, "Hey, Mister."

I turned to see a street kid walking toward me.

So I stood and waited for him.

"I heard your talk in there," he said, inclining his head toward the church.

"Oh?" I said.

"Yeah, and I just wanted to tell you I can't believe in God."

Feeling tired and unprepared to defend my faith in a sidewalk debate with someone who seemed to have already made up his mind, I needed time to plot my argument. So I stalled by asking, "Why don't you tell me about the God you don't believe in? Maybe I don't believe in him either."

My challenger jumped on my question by saying he couldn't believe in a God who blessed the rich people in the country and never did anything for the poor, who sent awful diseases like cancer to punish innocent people, who condoned the racism of governments and institutions, who callously watched as the people of the world destroyed each other with wars. His list went on and on.

When he stopped, I told him I couldn't believe in a God like that either. Then I spent some time trying to explain what I thought was a biblical image of God we could agree on.

I didn't change my adversary's mind that day. But I believe I started him thinking. I know he started me thinking.

As a result of that encounter, and many others like it, I've come to the disturbing conclusion that millions of people are going through life believing or not believing in a God they have only a fuzzy, snapshot picture of.

I think we all need to ask ourselves the question, "What do I believe about God?"

I'm convinced it's the most important question we will ever ask. And it's the question we will look at in Part I of this book.

There is a point beyond which your mind cannot take you.

Ed Lallo

1

Why Should I Believe in a God?

Why do I believe in a God? Let me tell you a story.

Once upon a time, someone parachuted a wrist watch into a remote tribal village in Sumatra. He did it at night, so the villagers, who had never contacted civilization, only heard a tremendous, frightening roar pass over. The next morning a tribesman peeked out of his hut to find the watch lying there.

None of the villagers had seen anything like it; they gathered around jabbering and pointing, calling others to see the curious object.

After minutes of poking and looking, someone got the courage to pick it up. He smiled—it was smooth and cool to the touch, more so than any stone polished by a stream. He held it to his ear and let out an amazed yell—it ticked! Others grabbed it from his hand so they could listen as well.

Of course, people had work to do, and not everyone sat around looking at the watch. But there were some whose work was so well organized they had the free time to sit and pass it back and forth, studying its properties. There was a lot to study.

The watch stayed in the tribe for many years, and gradually many pieces of information were discovered about it. Fairly early, someone noticed that one of the hands went around in a circle. A little later someone realized that every time that hand went around once, another hand moved one click! That led to an even more astonishing discovery (which took years)—when that hand clicked all the way around once, the smallest hand moved from one marking to the next. When that smallest hand had passed all the markings twice, the sun came up!

Evidently, the sun and the watch worked together. Perhaps it was the watch that made the sun come up! Could it be their tribe had found the regulator of the universe? That theory was strengthened when someone discovered that the moon, in a very complicated way, was also linked to the watch.

People were a bit afraid of the watch. They remembered the terrifying roar that had accompanied its coming, and lots of theories were developed to explain its origin. Some said a giant wasp had dropped it. Others suggested it came from a flying lion, roaring through the heavens. Out of fear, some wanted to put the watch in a special strongbox, where only the witch doctor would look at it. They were afraid of it because they thought it controlled the sun and moon, and the idea of a giant wasp or flying lion was not very comforting.

Another group was less afraid, more interested in studying the watch. They felt that by careful examination they could discover something about the maker; they weren't sold on the flying lion theory. And they noticed many things.

First of all, the watch was symmetrical and predictable, not random. Second, it was durable—the maker must have had a concern for durability and function. Third, it was beautiful—it shone more than anything they had seen. The maker must love beauty. They concluded that the roaring lion theory, at least as it had been put forward, was wrong. Lions aren't too concerned with beauty or with order. But having given up the roaring lion theory, these village scientists developed a powerful curiosity about what *had* made it. The maker must be very powerful. He must have a powerful understanding of the totality of the universe, to link a small shiny object to the sun and moon. And he must be interested in order and beauty.

Curiously, not one tribesman in the whole village ever suggested that no one had made the watch—that it had just come into being by happenstance.

A World Like a Watch

If we look at our world, we'll find some strong similarities to the watch. First, it's orderly. There is some controversy in physics whether at the basic level things behave randomly or not, but at the level of astronomy there's no real argument. You can tell what time the sun will come up fifty years from today—it's very predictable.

And the earth is durable. It can be damaged, of course, but it doesn't occasionally go zinging toward the sun or threaten to crumble suddenly. We've been here for thousands of years and discovered ecology only a few years ago—the earth must be fairly durable to survive thousands of years of people mining it, digging canals, exploding bombs, building fires, and killing animals. And obviously, the world is beautiful—far more beautiful than any work the greatest artist has ever done.

Down through history, most people have looked at the wonder of creation and concluded that, like the watch, the world must have a maker. Philosophers call this kind of logic the argument from design.

There are limits to this kind of argument. Different people can look at the same results and come to very different conclusions about what God is like. Remember the roaring lion theory? For example, some people look at the balance of elements and chemicals that make life possible and conclude that the creator was a consistent, trustworthy lover of order. Other people look at hurricanes and volcanoes and decide the creator of the world must be whimsical, unpredictable, and even fond of disorder. So we don't always get a completely accurate picture of God from his creation; the world is not a mirror of him. That's why God gave us other evidence about what he's like—evidence we'll examine in later chapters.

But creation is still one valid yardstick for measuring part of God. And it is reasonable to look at the incredible world around us and conclude, as most people have until the last hundred years or so, that there has to be someone behind it all. A creator.

Recently, however, there are some people suggesting what the villagers never imagined—that there is no maker, that the world just happened. The argument goes, if you don't mind my simplifying, like this: We understand how the world works in the minutest detail. We can explain and even duplicate many things that baffled our forefathers. Therefore, there is no God. Belief in him is outmoded; we don't need him to explain things.

That argument sounds suspiciously like this one: My father built a house. I studied the house, and learned how it is made. I can now build a house. Therefore my father did not exist.

I'm just making the point that most people, confronted with a something similar to our earth, would assume a maker was responsible. The more modern science discovers about our incredible world, the harder it is to believe otherwise.

If you read Romans 1:18–23, you find this basic thought: that everyone can know there is a God by looking at the world. Not only that, though. Paul claims you can know something about the character of God. In other words, he says the universe itself is grounds for knowing that the maker is not fierce and amoral like a roaring lion or giant wasp. But why does he say that?

Right and Wrong

Part of his reasoning must be based on the order, durability, and beauty of the world. I think it goes beyond that, however. We can say we know the Creator cares about whether we do right or wrong.

Why Believe in Jesus?

Why? Because included in what the Creator made are human beings. They always care about right and wrong. Their societies always have rules. Some of those rules are simply good sense for preservation, but some are constructed to protect the weak from the strong. There are very few societies where it is considered good to betray a friend. Sooner or later, when people argue politics or law, you hear someone say something like, "We ought not to do that." But why not? Simply because there is something built into us that holds to right and wrong.

Right and wrong aren't just a frill, either; they're basic. If you're in the hands of torturers who think nothing of killing you or making you suffer inconceivably, you have only one power. But it is a great power. Deep in your soul you can say, "I am right. I am on the side of truth."

Solzhenitsyn, in writing of the terror of brutal torture in Soviet prison camps, wrote this:

> So what is the answer? How can you stand your ground when you are weak and sensitive to pain, when people you love are still alive, when you are unprepared?
>
> What do you need to make you stronger than the interrogator and the whole trap?
>
> From the moment you go to prison you must put your cozy past firmly behind you. At the very threshold, you must say to yourself: "My life is over, a little early to be sure, but there's nothing to be done about it. I shall never return to freedom. I am condemned to die—now or a little later. But later on, in truth, it will be even harder, and so the sooner the better. I no longer have any property whatsoever. For me those I love have died, and for them I have died. From today on, my body is useless and alien to me. Only my spirit and my conscience remain precious and important to me."

ISBN Cat. No.

0-310 0-310711191-6 14119P

Title:

MAKING LIFE MAKE SEN

KESLER/

REG. PRICE 6.95

OUR PRICE 595

Store Name:

OVERLAKE CHRISTIAN BOOK STORE

Account No.	070640
Invoice No.	6187684
Invoice Date	4/03/91
P.O. No.	022691

Re-Order Qty. ______________

To Re-Order Call 1-800-727-1309

000004-4200-0000695-0000000-

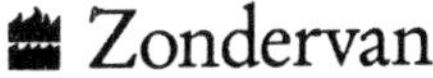

A Division of HarperCollinsPublishers

> Confronted by such a prisoner, the interrogater will tremble.
>
> Only the man who has renounced everything can win that victory.*

There is tremendous power in the person who holds on to his conscience when everything else is gone. Why? Because everyone—even his torturer—knows inside that something is right and something wrong. It seems a fair assumption that whoever or whatever made him holds that same standard. We call that maker "God."

Christians Say More

This is a basic idea of Christianity. It is also the basic idea behind most other religions. However, when people say, "All religions teach the same thing," they couldn't be much more wrong. The different religions have vastly different ways of looking at the world and come to some very diverse conclusions. But in one respect most are largely in agreement: There is a God who controls the world, and we ought to please him.

But how to please him? Most religions suggest that by learning truth and obeying rules, by meditating or attending worship, man raises himself to a place where he can contact God. Christians hold that is impossible. God is so high that trying to raise ourselves to reach him is like standing on someone's shoulders to touch the moon. Instead, Christains claim that God has come down to us.

So any argument about God's existence or believability must eventually lead to Jesus Christ himself. Jesus did exist in history; he is not a mythical figure. We have original historical documents written by eyewitnesses. It is amazing to me how many people who argue against Christianity's God have never even read those documents. They argue on the basis of a misty memory of

---

*Alexander Solzhenitsyn, *The Gulag Archipelago, 1918–1956: An Experiment in Literary Investigation* (New York: Harper & Row, 1974), p. 130.

Sunday school combined with something they heard in a history class. The source documents are easy to get, but they've never bothered! It's as though someone were arguing that Shakespeare's plays were not especially good, and you discovered during the argument that he'd never read any of them.

Just on the basis of intellectual honesty we should go to the New Testament and find out the facts. We can encourage those people to confront Jesus Christ and what he was really like. After all, Christianity stands or falls on the basis of whether Jesus was really God; shouldn't we all get away from our images of him and discover whether he really measures up to what's claimed?

When you read the New Testament, you don't see Jesus as simply a wise teacher or the original pacifist. What strikes you first of all is his audacity. He isn't the head of anything, and he goes around trailed by the dregs of humanity. Yet he talks as though he's king! He doesn't care what people think of him, yet he's not arrogant; he's humble enough to care about the smallest, saddest person in the crowd. The truth he speaks is irrefutable; the wisest men are left sputtering. Yet he talks about his "kingdom" and even when they take him to the real king, who can have him killed by flicking his finger, Jesus acts more as though the tables were reversed and the king was *his* subject. Even death, according to the New Testament, could not rule over him; he won the battle with it and came back to life.

Read the New Testament, and see if Jesus is a person you can conveniently label "great teacher." If he was a great teacher and nothing more, why does he talk the way he does? The best teacher in your school would soon be carted away if he started talking about his "kingdom," intimating that he had a special, unique relationship to God, that in fact he and God the Father "are one," and saying he was the only road to God. As C. S. Lewis pointed out, Jesus was either a fraud, as crazy as a man who thinks he's a poached egg, or he was what he said he was.

Of course, some suggest that the writers of the New Testament hedged on the truth quite a bit in order to make a religion out of it. A lot of people have spent time trying to separate the real Jesus from what was added later on. The idea that Jesus rose again from the dead has been a chief target.

But what happened to those New Testament writers? In every case we know of, history records that the disciples died for what they believed. Remember, Christianity was not the popular thing when it started. You could be killed for believing it, and many were. People don't usually die defending something they know is a lie—especially when the very cause they're dying for places a high premium on telling the truth. If you're going to die for something, you want to get the facts straight.

Skywriting Proof?

I've given you some of the best reasons I know for believing in a God. There are plenty of other ways to argue for the same thing: by looking at how Bible prophecies came true, or how archaeology validates the Bible. Any of these evidences could possibly tip the scales in favor of belief. If you're looking for proof, however—proof as tangible and obvious as skywriting—you won't find it. The arguments that God exists and Christianity is true are strong ones; I've sketched them here, and if you're interested in more depth you should read something like C. S. Lewis's *Mere Christianity*. But intelligent, honest people disbelieve. Sometimes you might hear a Christian speaker talk about evidence in favor of Christianity with such power you're absolutely sure there's no debating it. You leave saying inside, "Gotcha!" However, I can assure you there are intelligent people who build a powerful case in the opposite direction. It depends a lot on who holds the microphone.

Are we caught in the middle, tempted to throw away all arguments, pro and con? Should we stop using our minds and "just believe"? No. We ought to use our minds to their utmost, and then "just believe." For there is a point beyond which your mind cannot take you. After you've gone through all the intellectual questions about Christianity, there is still a choice to be made. It is a choice of faith. It is a decision about who you will ultimately trust, and about what kind of life you believe in your heart is right.

I can remember speaking at a college once, and afterwards walking home with one of the professors. He didn't believe in Christ, but he seemed to be honestly searching. He had many, many questions. There wasn't time to answer them all, and when we parted he said, with deep feeling, "Pray for me, Jay. I want to believe, but I can't."

The Impossible Dream

Non-Christians aren't always people in angry, sarcastic, argumentative rebellion against God. I find many like that professor, wanting to believe but not seeing that it is possible. For them, it's important first to show that God is believable—that there is a good basis for accepting as genuine what Christ said. And perhaps they have special questions that need to be answered; this professor was a scientist and needed to be shown (probably by other scientists; through books) that there was no necessary contradiction between science and a belief in God.

But those answers are not enough. The scientist would have to see that there was more to life than science. There are mysteries beyond the atom. Every relationship, for example, is a deep mystery. There is no pill or treatment for loneliness. There is no way to penetrate the life of a person who will not let you love him or her. Sociology, psychology, physics, or biology are useless when you are trying to help someone who will not be helped, or trying to change your own self so you'll stop hurting people. There is a deep reality of sin in human beings. But there is also a deep appreciation of beauty, of truth, of love. Life is a hopelessly complicated, contradictory picture with countless gaps and unanswered questions.

But there are answers. The complete picture does make sense. A belief in God is like the cover photo on the front of a puzzle box; it shows how everything is supposed to fit together.

Of course, knowing what the photo of a jigsaw puzzle looks like doesn't mean you instantly solve the whole puzzle. You can often get stuck on one central piece. Until you get that piece, nothing works. You may try to force the wrong piece in, or even whittle a little bit of it away to make it fit. But when you have the right piece, all the others begin to fall in place—not instantly, not easily—but they do fall in place.

Archimedes wrote that "if you give me a lever and a place to stand, I can move the world." Elton Trueblood, in the book *A Place to Stand,* uses that idea to say that Jesus Christ is the place to stand—a center from which the other pieces of your world can be moved.

So much of the Christian message seems, on experience, consistent with the way the world is. For example, Christianity has always said people are sinful; now, after years of the world's denying it, the famous Karl Menninger writes a book called *Whatever Happened to Sin?* Christianity, he concludes, was right after all. The pieces seem to fit. There are other ways of looking at the world, but the pieces keep having to be moved and changed. They don't fit right.

Ultimately, if you're considering whether or not to believe in God, you aren't confronted with ideas alone. You're confronted with God himself. It's a very personal decision—who will you believe? Who will you trust? No one can ever prove to you conclusively, in advance, that faith in God will satisfy you. Certainly faith in God will never turn out to bring exactly the rewards you hoped, because we never manage to understand God completely. His thoughts are bigger than ours; his plans are bigger than ours.

Ultimately you must choose, not because some Christian argues you to the point of giving up, but because God confronts you—in the person of Jesus Christ. He can't be ignored. You have to turn toward him, or else turn away. The arguments in his favor, though powerful, won't take you to true faith. In my own life, it was a question of trust—whom I would rely on. I chose God.

TAKEOFF

If you were going to try to convince a friend of the existence of God by pointing out evidence you see in creation, what would you use as your most powerful arguments?

Spend an hour walking outdoors. During that time, concentrate on the bits of creation you see around you. Make a list of conclusions you would draw about God from what you observe. When you're done, go back through the list and thank God for each of those parts of his creation and for its particular clue about his character.

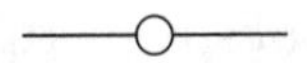

The most direct view the Bible offers of God as creator is found in Genesis 1 and 2. You can see a slightly different picture in John 1:1–14. And a number of the psalms are written as celebration of God's creativity: see Psalms 8, 19, 24, 104, 135, 148, and 150.

When he wants us to understand what he's like, God uses one universal image.

Jim Whitmer

2

If I Do Believe in God, How Can I Know What He's Like?

Frank was a guy who really cared about life. He had taken lots of drugs, but not for kicks. He was trying to get hold of life—trying to make the puzzle fit together by making sense of himself, the world, and God. When I talked to him, I sensed that seriousness immediately. He listened very carefully.

"But Jay," he said, "I can't grasp the idea of God. Every time I think I'm getting closer, I find out he isn't where I thought he was. It's like someone's taken an ice cream stick and scraped out his insides until there's just skin. But that's not right either. He doesn't even have a skin—at least not one I can touch."

I was tempted to pass it off as a cop-out, just another excuse for unbelief. But I saw he was serious. And when I thought about what he was saying, I realized it was a problem everyone faces. Jesus recognized it, I think, when he told Thomas, "You believe because you have seen me. But blessed are those who haven't seen me and believe anyway" (John 20:29).

That's the dilemma we face—under ordinary circumstances we don't see God. Even if you decide there is a

God to believe in, you can't feel him. You don't audibly hear his voice. So when you want to know him and understand him, you have a problem. That's why there are so many misconceptions like those mentioned in chapter 1—incomplete and wrong ideas of what God is like.

If we're not careful, we end up with a God who is nothing more than the sum of our experiences. This is what primitive man does. Every time he has an experience he goes out and carves a face on his totem pole. A tornado wipes out his house and he carves a big scowling face. A flood comes, same thing. Pretty soon he has a totem pole stacked with scowling faces; he has developed a hostile, frightening image of God.

Things are different in our time. Science and technology make most of us safe from catastrophes. They put a roof over our heads and food in our stomachs. So the faces we carve on our totem pole are smiling. We get a good grade, God is smiling. We find a parking place, God is smiling. But this image of God isn't any more valuable than the scowling one, because it's still based only on experience. If our closest friend dies, or we flunk a few classes, the faces on the totem pole may change expressions. We need to get beyond our day-to-day experiences with nature and environment to discover the real God who made all these objects.

Misconceptions have always existed. In the first century, when Jesus lived, you might have had a strange idea of what God was like. In China or in Rome, you might have thought he was the emperor. If you wanted to get handles on God in Scandinavia two thousand years ago, you put a maiden on a ship with some fruits and vegetables, and sent her out to sea. When the sea devoured her, you would think that you had seen God at work. In Germany you might have offered a young maiden, too—perhaps burned her at the stake. In the British Isles you might have participated in a cannibalistic ritual. On the Easter Islands you might have carved a huge stone statue.

These may seem like ridiculous ways to get in touch with God, but when you've posed the question, "How do you get in touch with God?" where would you go to find a sensible answer? The answer to that question depends on your picture of God. And I'm not sure that picture is much clearer in our day.

In fact, I'd bet the average twentieth-century person, if he told you what he really thinks God is like, would come up with many of the ancient misconceptions. I think he'd say, for one thing, that God is harsh—that he's made up ten thousand sins that we can't avoid because of the natural desires and drives he's given us, and he's just waiting to catch us disobeying the rules so he can wipe us out. People still think God likes punishing people every chance he gets.

I suspect most people would also say that God is very distant. He's high up in his heaven, and we're small and insignificant—and that's the way God keeps it. If he'd let the sky crack at all so you could see him up there, he'd look like a combination of a lightning bolt and Mr. Clean. Not the sort of God you'd want to get close to or talk to about your problems.

A Surprising Model

Jesus' disciples had similar ideas. True, they were Jewish, and so they had some good Old Testament ideas of what God was like. But there were still problems for them. That's why they came to Jesus asking, "Lord, teach us how to pray." What they were really saying was, "How can we communicate with God? How can we understand him?" And Jesus answered in a startling way. He broke through many centuries of stiffness. He taught them to begin their prayers by addressing God, "Our Father." He didn't say, "Most High and Holy Potentate, Omnipotent and All-Powerful." He began the Lord's Prayer, a model for all other prayers, with one of the most ordinary, familiar words in existence, "Father."

This familiar image offers a much clearer picture of God

than we get just from examining creation or our experiences with our environment. *We are the children; God is the father.* Just consider some implications of that idea.

It means first of all that God loves us. There is an intimacy between parent and child that doesn't exist in any other kind of relationship. (Unfortunately, all parents are less than perfect. This distorts what Jesus is saying a bit, for some people more than others. So, we can think about God as a father and still have an incomplete or wrong picture of what that means.)

There are, however, some easily understood implications in a father-child relationship. It is unique because the child doesn't have a choice in it. You're born with parents; you don't get to pick and choose. Yet you're inextricably tied together. Few things can tear a person up like a lousy relationship with parents. Few things can be more deeply meaningful than a loving, growing relationship with them.

That's a mere beginning image of the love we can have with our heavenly father, God. He is the most loving, consistent father possible. He looks at us, always, with the tenderness a father feels peeking into the cradle of his first baby.

But that's not all Jesus is implying. A father's love involves more than warm feelings of tenderness or physical affection. Love is not only a soft, gentle word; it's also a strong, powerful word. For a father, it's full of many meanings. Let me begin to explain with an example.

Crunched by a Car

My children had a rule that they couldn't ride their bikes in the street until they were eight years old. All the other neighborhood kids were riding in the street, but mine had to ride on the sidewalk. They didn't like it. They thought I was really old-fashioned, and when I told them I didn't want them to get hit by a car, they didn't understand my reasoning. They'd complain, and I'm pretty sure they'd sneak off on the street when I wasn't around. But then one day Terry came home and said, "Timmy got crunched by a car."

I said, "What do you mean, crunched by a car?"

She told me he'd been riding his bike in the street and a car hit him. I said, "Now do you understand why I don't want you to ride your bike in the street?"

"Yeah," she said. "You don't want me to get crunched by a car."

I think that's the essence of the Ten Commandments. God doesn't say, "Thou shalt not commit adultery," and "Thou shalt not steal," because he's trying to ruin our good times. He wants to protect our happiness, not take it away. But when our happiness destroys other people's happiness, then God, being the Father of the family, has to control it. He does it with rules, like any father. The Ten Commandments are like stop signs. They're not there to wreck our transmission or to increase our driving time. They're sort of an agreement: I'll stop, and you'll stop, and that way we don't kill each other.

This is why God isn't just all warm and fuzzy feelings. Sometimes he seems to bristle with rules. But they're rules with a purpose, because God, much more than our human fathers, really knows what's going on. He sees the future. He knows precisely the kind of person you are. He knows what things are really important in life.

God's discipline is not punishment. It's his way of trying to teach us boundaries, to keep us from being crunched or destroyed by life. And that discipline is just one of the results and evidences of God's love.

Discipline is related to another evidence of God's love—restraint. A father could easily break the spine of a tiny child with a single blow. But a loving father restrains his power, even in the act of discipline. Our heavenly Father is not a child abuser.

Think for a minute about the power of a volcano like Mt. St. Helens in Washington. A single explosion sent millions of tons of pulverized earth and rock scattering for hundreds of miles. I've heard some people say of Mt. St.

Helens, "That was only one small volcano. Just consider the incredible power God has."

A volcano does say something about the power of God. After all, the creator of volcanoes must be infinitely more powerful than his creations. But that kind of thinking provides only a limited view of what God is really like—by itself a distorted view. It makes me very grateful for the balancing analogy of God as a father whose love requires him to restrain his power. Without that restraint, his sense of justice would have obliterated the world long ago. The idea of restraint is a comforting, reassuring implication of fatherly love.

The love of a father also involves the element of provision. A loving father will do everything in his power to provide for the well-being of his children. Parental love means protection; a father's protectiveness has been a universal theme in literature since time began. And you could list many more evidences and implications of a father's love.

But there's one more aspect of fatherhood that probably wouldn't occur to you, because our society is different from Jesus'. Jesus came from a strong Jewish family, and for the Jews the father was always—for all of life—the most important person. You didn't get away from him just by going away to college. In all probability you lived in the same house with him your whole life. The oldest man in the family always spoke first. There was deep respect and reverence for him.

The same thing is true of God. You don't lightly call him by his first name. You don't kick him out of the house when you're tired of him. You can never really leave him behind when you go away to college or get married. He's always there and always demands to be treated with great respect and reverence. He's not your buddy; he's your Father—your link with all the wisdom and understanding there is in the universe.

One other thing about fathers ties into this. Because your father isn't your buddy (or at least wasn't in a Jewish home), you might not go to him for every little problem. But when you run up against problems you can't solve yourself, you want to talk to someone with a little more ability to help—someone with enough experience and power to understand. Then you go to your father. That is the way God is with us. Let's face it, there are problems we can hassle out ourselves. But when things are really on the edge of despair, we need a Father in heaven who is ready to listen and help.

How can I know what God's like? God doesn't have a skin. He doesn't give us something tangible we can physically hold onto. But he does give us an image we can grab onto and hold, no matter how we're feeling: God is our Father.

That's a truth I can understand and stake my life on.

TAKEOFF

Make a list of adjectives you think would describe the perfect father. Which ones best fit your image of God?

Try to think of two or three other analogies (besides *father*) you might use to explain the nature of God to a friend. Compare those images with Jesus' image of God as father. What image would you use if you were trying to explain God to a small child whose father beat her and her mother before finally deserting his family?

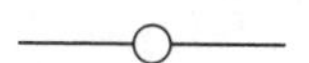

You'll find a lot of study in the Bible if you want to get a picture of God as a father. The whole Old Testament is the story of God the father and his children of Israel. But the New Testament helps bring the image into clearer focus. The most obvious passage to check out is the story of the Prodigal Son in Luke 15. But Jesus' attitude toward his father is also seen in his prayer in Matthew 6:5–15.

Jesus came to prove we don't have to be superhuman to live the life we were meant to live.

Rick Smolan

3

How Does Jesus Fit In?

Creation gives us a picture of God. And the simple word *Father* conveys profound truth about him. But the universe and a simple human analogy as presented in the Old Testament were not enough. They didn't give a complete enough picture of God for us to understand him in the way he wanted to be understood.

So God took one more huge step toward mankind by initiating the greatest contact of all time between himself and us—the sending of his own Son, Jesus Christ, to earth. The result was a face-to-face, close-up view of God himself.

Exactly the Right Time

When most people think of Jesus' coming, they think of Christmas, camels, swaddling clothes, and a manger. But I like to think of a Ford Motor Plant. It tells me something about the great event we call Christmas.

One year I toured a plant and watched them assemble cars. It was an eye-opener. I'd always had the idea Ford would just guess how many cars they needed, and make that many. They'd decide to make green cars one day, and make two or three thousand. Then they'd switch to some other color.

But that's not the way they do it. All over America people walk into Ford dealerships, look around, kick a few tires, and then order a car—a certain model with specific equipment, color, roof, transmission, and defroster. The dealer fills out a computer card and an order is placed with Ford. In one city they make the correct transmission, and in another city they make vinyl roofs, and in another, mirrors. All these places start feeding their products toward the Ford plant.

The Ford plant has a man who puts on steering wheels. The cars come down the line, and when the green cars come you can bet he doesn't get a red steering wheel to put on. At exactly the right time, the green steering wheels are there. He reaches out, grabs one, and sticks it on. That's what happens with each part—the mirror, the roof, the seat covers—every part shows up at precisely the right instant.

Now if man is capable of designing such an ingenious system to bring thousands of events and people together with precision timing just to make a car, imagine what God can do in preparing for his visit to earth. That's what I think of at Christmas—the number of things God brought together at one time in one place is so incredible, it makes the Ford plant look like the corner gas station.

The Scheme of Things

Some people have the idea that Jesus was a remedial action, a last minute Band-Aid stuck on a wounded world. God had unsuccessfully tried everything else, so he decided to try his Son. But the Bible says Jesus came in the fullness of time—when everything was as fully prepared for him as possible. All the pieces of history fell together.

The preparation God did is staggering. God had used a man named Alexander to conquer the entire known world and spread Greek as a language for practically every educated person. The good news about Jesus Christ could spread without language barriers because of that.

Then came the Roman Empire—a government that just happened to build good roads throughout the known world so that travel was easy—again, providing an easier way for the gospel to spread. And think of the thousands of years God had worked with the Jewish people, opening up their understanding of him so they were ready for the things Jesus said and did.

God had spent thousands of years getting ready to come! All his preparation culminated in a single, incongruous event—a baby born to noninfluential people in a rural town of a small, conquered nation. The only fanfare for the greatest event in history was heard by a bunch of no-account shepherds.

Jesus Was No Superman

Now, what do you make of that? All that preparation, yet no publicity at the actual event. Isn't that like preparing a senior banquet for months and then forgetting to send out invitations?

Not if you see the point. The wise men, the shepherds, the manger—those weren't just thrown into the story for local color. They hint at other fantastic things about how God treats the world—things you might never guess.

When people through the ages have thought about how God might come to earth, most of the time they've thought of him coming down in a chariot of fire to do some fantastic thing—kind of a religious Superman. You find this idea in most of the early religions—the Roman and Greek and Phoenician mythologies.

But Mary and Joseph were just poor young people. A carpenter then was probably about as prestigious as a carpenter now. Christmas makes the point that God deliberately sent his Son to the humblest of people. By sending his Son to people like that, God was telling us he isn't concerned about how much money you make or how many people know your name. No matter how unimportant everybody else thinks you are, he doesn't think so. It was your kind of people that he chose as parents for his Son. Not only was he willing to visit them, he was willing to become one of them. Jesus came as a human baby, not as some comic book super hero—faster than a speeding bullet, more powerful than a locomotive.

This idea is hard to grasp. God becoming a helpless baby! Jesus was one of us! He grew up and went through the same kinds of problems we go through. The Bible says he was tempted in every way we're tempted. That means, for instance, he must have been sexually tempted. He had to work at controlling his impulses just as we do. If he didn't, then Jesus was hollow. He looked like a man on the outside, but if he wasn't really tempted, his insides were empty of the problems we face.

But Jesus wasn't a hollow man. He gave up his privileges as God and became a man. He was living proof that you don't have to be superhuman to live the kind of life you were meant to. You just have to be obedient to God.

Sometimes I wish I could solve all my problems by magic, just whisk them away. But Jesus, with all the power of God, didn't handle his own troubles that way. He faced them head-on. So I know I'm going to have to face my problems in the same way. What's more, I know it's possible to face them with Jesus and come out on top. Because Jesus stayed perfect using the same weapons I have at my disposal.

Moving Up Alongside the World

God came to earth as a man so we'd have a realistic model to follow. But there's another reason. To saddle a horse, you put your hand on him slowly and move it gently up his side. Gradually you move up alongside him so that he's used to you, and then you put the saddle on. That way you don't spook the horse.

In a sense that's what God was doing in Bethlehem. He was moving up the side of mankind slowly so we wouldn't get all tense. He wanted to do some things that wouldn't be possible from a fiery chariot. God wanted to identify with man, not give him advice. If he'd wanted to give advice, he could have done it with a bullhorn from heaven. Instead he came as a child. Even the most timid person isn't afraid of an infant.

And when Jesus did exciting things, they didn't necessarily seem exciting. Jesus was moving up slowly. If you look back at the events in the New Testament, you could say, Wow! and try to synthetically reproduce the excitement in your own life. If you did, you'd be frustrated. Take the Christmas scene for instance. Spectacular? As far as everybody in town was concerned, nothing was happening. People were standing in line to make out their tax returns, pushing and shoving.

Everybody was trying to find a place to stay for the night, and one unfortunate young couple couldn't squeeze in. The guy in charge of the local hotel generously tried to provide a place by clearing out a stable, and Joseph saw it was better than sleeping outside, so he took it. Sure a baby was born there, but in those days, where were most of the babies born? People were having them in tents out in the desert. It probably wasn't too unusual. As far as everybody around was concerned, that was a ho-hum night.

That's the way God is working now. There are lots of things around that appear ho-hum, but are really spectacular if you dig deep. Answered prayer, for instance. Sometimes when God answers, I'm prompted to say, "Big deal. Maybe it was a coincidence." Or somebody becoming a Christian. To the neighborhood maybe it isn't even worth yawning about. But to those inside, with eyes to see, it's the greatest miracle of all.

The Original Pattern

We are to imitate Jesus in our lives. He is the pattern we are to live by. But we need to make sure we're dealing with the real pattern, not some illusion we've built up. What really happened back then? If we know that, then we can act consistently with it.

My dad tells a story about building a barn for a man whose barn had burned. All the people in the neighborhood came together and assigned certain guys to cut the rafters. All these guys had to do was follow a pattern.

But instead of using the original pattern for each rafter that was to be cut, they would mark one, cut it, and then use it to mark the next one, and so on. Each time they marked a rafter, however, they were gaining just one pencil width in length. Each marking would only add 1/32 of an inch or so at each end. It doesn't amount to much, except they kept compounding it until they were one-half inch off on the sixteenth rafter. By the thirty-second rafter they were one inch off its pattern. Eventually they realized their error and had to recut all the rafters.

Some of us are in that position when it comes to following Jesus—we copy something somebody told us or some feeling we remember, and we miss the mark.

This is why the Bible goes to such pains to tell us what Jesus was really like. He is the pattern we're supposed to live by. The person who wants to follow Christ has to keep going back to that original pattern.

I particularly stress the Bible, God's Word. The psalmist wrote, "How can a young man stay pure? By reading your Word and following its rules. I have thought much about your words, and stored them in my heart so that they would hold me back from sin" (Ps. 119:8, 11). There are certain habits of Bible study and prayer which lead you back to the original pattern of Jesus Christ. I put a high priority on developing those habits. I've learned not to make all kinds of lofty ideals for myself, but to think of practical vows like, "I will not go to bed at night without reading from the Bible." A morning person might say, "I won't start the day without Bible reading and prayer."

Here's a formula that has helped me. I begin by bowing and acknowledging God and his control of my life. I ask him to teach me one specific thing from his Word. Then, as soon as something specific jumps out, and the Spirit seems to underline it in my mind, I stop right there and meditate on it. I ask God to add that particular virtue to my life.

That doesn't sound like much—but suppose I learned one lesson a day. That would be 365 lessons in a year. In ten years it would be over 3,650—quite a few lessons to learn from the original pattern.

How does Jesus fit in? He is the final step in God's revelation of himself to mankind. He came to put a face on God. More than that, he showed us how we can relate to God and live the kind of life he wants us to live. Because Christ came to earth, we know better than ever what God the Creator and Father is like. We know without a doubt that God cared about us. And we know that God can help us with our problems.

We know all this because God has been where we are.

TAKEOFF

Suppose you're a senior partner of a giant public relations firm and God decides to hire your services. He says he wants to prove his love to the world and show what he's like once and for all. He's decided the best way to do it is to send his Son to the world as his personal representative to carry his message. He wants your firm to propose the best strategy for getting the most exposure for his message. What would you suggest? Take a few minutes to think about the possibilities. Remember, your resources are unlimited.

Compare your PR plan with God's strategy. What does that tell you about God's values?

Make a list of the characteristics of Jesus that most impress you.

———o———

You can read about God's plan, as foretold centuries before it was carried out, by looking up Isaiah 53. And of course the details were recorded in the accounts of the Christmas story in Luke 2 and Matthew 2. John 1:6–22 also talks about the purpose of Jesus' coming.

When you love someone
and you know him or her well,
you know things are right.

Steve Wall

4

What Does It Mean to Know God Personally?

In college I once had the honor of being chairman of a religious emphasis week. The college brought in a speaker, and he was introduced to the faculty in a special meeting. I was the only student there. It was an imposing situation, because, naturally, everyone was older and far more educated than I. But somehow in the course of discussion I mentioned that I prayed and that I knew God heard me pray.

To give the faculty credit, they didn't just pass it off with an amused smile. They listened and questioned me. "How do you know God hears you? How do you know you're not just talking into the air?"

If I were asked that now I might say some things about the character of God—that he is not the kind of God who doesn't listen. But perhaps my answer then was just as effective. "Well, I just *know*. The Spirit bears witness with my spirit that I'm a child of God."

"Well," someone said, "you could be undergoing some sort of psychological experience, imagining a response from God that isn't objectively there at all."

I didn't know what to say. I remember looking desperately around the room at the faces of those alert, intelligent men and women I respected so much. I saw one of the profs I knew rather well. His wife was with him. "Doctor," I asked, "do you love your wife?"

"Yes," he said.

Then I turned to his wife. "Do you love your husband?" She said yes also.

I turned back to the prof. "How do you know she loves you?"

He said, "She tells me so."

I asked his wife, and she said the same thing.

I said, "You know, you could be lying to each other. You think everything's fine, but, Doctor, your wife could be carrying on on the side. She might be *saying* all those things about love just to keep you from knowing the truth."

"No," he said, "when you love someone and you know her well, you know things are right."

"Well," I said, "it's the same thing between God and me. There's a communication that goes beyond words when you love someone."

I realize now that you can overstress that intimate aspect of relating to Christ. Still, it's basic; Christianity is not a dry collection of facts about God. Christians don't simply know *about* God, they know *him*. When the Bible talks about that personal involvement, it talks about the Holy Spirit.

There are many pitfalls in trying to define the Holy Spirit. People have killed each other arguing over definitions of the Trinity—of God the Father, the Son, and the Holy Spirit. I don't intend to get involved in that controversy. It's clear to me, though, that when we talk about the direct communication of God to man, we're talking about the Holy Spirit. The Spirit is a way in which God, not using a physical body, can exist in the world and communicate with his own people, yet not destroy their independence.

Before Jesus left our planet, he promised that he would

send the Holy Spirit. In fact, he said it was *better* for us if he left, because otherwise the Holy Spirit would not come. Now why was it better? A lot of people look back on the disciples and figure, "Man, if I'd been with them, it would have been easy. I could have physically seen and touched Jesus. My faith would never waver."

But suppose Jesus was here, physically, today. He could be only one place at one time. Probably he'd stay in Jerusalem, and you'd have to save your money to take a once-in-a-lifetime excursion to see him. Once you arrived, you'd have to fight the crowds. Perhaps, if you were lucky, you'd get in to see him with a group of others. He might say a few words, wave to everyone, and shake hands with a few. He would answer a couple of questions. Naturally, there wouldn't be time for everyone's questions. Reporters and photographers would mill around. Then the time would be up and you'd be ushered out, and the next group would come in to see him.

For the rest of your life you'd try to remember that moment. But your memory would fade, and you'd lose touch with him. Furthermore, you might not have a complete picture. If you saw him on a day similar to the day he chased the money changers out of the temple, your view would be different from "Let the little children come to me, for of such is the kingdom of God."

But because we have the Holy Spirit, we don't have these problems. The Spirit is Christ speaking to each of us at any time. He is not limited by geography. And because he speaks to us through the Bible, we get a balanced point of view. Our encounter with Jesus Christ isn't limited to a few moments; it takes in hundreds of the most important things he did and said in his life.

I don't think there's anything in Christianity more exciting and joyful than the doctrine of the Holy Spirit. It means that I'm special to God. God is not content to give himself to the masses; he wants to give himself to me. He wants to know me. He wants to help *me* as I struggle my way through life.

Grasshopper God

Unfortunately, we can't talk about the Holy Spirit without getting rid of some misconceptions. For many of us, the Holy Spirit has become not a loving person, but a thing.

My worst experience of this came in a small community. I was speaking there for a week. After the first meeting one sane-appearing, middle-aged man came up and said, "You know, in this community you're going to find that things are a little different."

I said, "How's that?"

"Well, in this community the Holy Spirit is a jumper."

"A jumper?" I said.

"Well, yeah, he'll be at one church for a while, and then he'll jump over to another church. I've watched it over the years. He just jumps from church to church."

I hardly knew where to start with the guy. He apparently envisioned the Holy Spirit as a large grasshopper.

You won't find too many people talking about the Holy Spirit as a "jumper," but you can find many misconceptions of the Holy Spirit. And two of the most common tendencies, when combined, result in something as far off base as a Holy Ghost grasshopper.

The first misconception comes from trying to visualize the Holy Spirit. He's invisible, but the way most of our minds work, we don't totally accept that. Some of our ideas come from the movies. I remember in *The Ten Commandments* Cecil B. De Mille portrayed the Spirit of the Lord as a dark fog coming down the street, killing the baby Egyptians. Some of us have a "fog" image of the Holy Spirit.

Or the Spirit is a little man about the size of a statue riding on someone's dashboard who "lives inside our hearts."

To a degree, these images are inevitable and harmless. But they are certainly not very personable, are they?

We need to come back, in all our thinking, to the fact

that the Spirit is a person. He is, in fact, Jesus Christ, speaking to us individually and personally.

Since the Holy Spirit is a person, we expect to see him affecting people differently from a force or an object. Forces push you around; a person who loves you can affect your whole personality, but he does it subtly, lovingly. And that's how the Holy Spirit works in our lives—like a friend. He's a person, not a thing.

The other misconception is more subtle, but it's dangerous too. We sing the song, "There's a sweet, sweet Spirit in this place, and I know it is the Spirit of the Lord." In a sense, that's right, because when Christians are gathered together to worship God and sing, the feelings they share *are* prompted by the presence of God. The danger is in thinking that there's no difference between a group spirit and the Holy Spirit.

You know, if you're feeling lousy, it doesn't mean the Spirit has left you. That's when he wants to comfort you.

If we think the Spirit is nothing more than a group spirit, we go around constantly looking for the group that's "on fire." But the Holy Spirit doesn't follow good feelings around like a dog on a leash. He's to be found wherever Christians are, not wherever good feelings are. You can create a certain atmosphere, or spirit, but that doesn't mean it has much depth or that the Spirit of God is particularly involved.

The man who thought the Holy Spirit was a "jumper" evidently thought you could track the Holy Spirit by following the path of excitement. Probably every time a church got excited, someone said, "You can really feel the Spirit." Well, the Holy Spirit is exciting at times. But he's also a "still, small voice" that isn't spectacular at all. And he's present when a single individual stands out against greed and oppression and is laughed at for his pains.

Your Mind Matters

If you wrote down everything the Bible says about the Holy Spirit, and took time to talk about each thing, you would have a long book. I'd rather talk about a few of the things that seem most important to our generation.

Let's start by talking about what business the Holy Spirit is in. We think, sometimes, that the Holy Spirit is a kind of tool we use to get things from God. If we treat him right, we think, we'll get what we want. Or we use him as a stamp of approval on what we believe, or on our good feelings. "The Spirit told me this, so I did it." But the Holy Spirit is really here to teach me about Christ. He always shows off Christ, never himself, and he is helping us understand and live the full, balanced truth about God and ourselves.

That's why Martin Luther and many others in the Reformation came up with a very important principle, which they called "Spirit and Word." They said the Spirit never works where the Bible is not at work. And the Bible never works in people's lives unless the Spirit is there. If you find one, you're bound to find the other.

Now this doesn't mean that the Bible is a kind of fourth part of the Trinity. It just means that the Spirit consistently uses the Word. He wants to communicate to us, he wants to do it clearly and without stuttering, and he wants to speak so that everyone will be able to understand, not just a few. We believe God gave us the Bible to do those very things.

Therefore, the Spirit is never involved with turning off your mind. You can't turn off your mind and turn up your emotions and then really understand the Bible. Yes, you can read the Bible like a comic strip, catching a verse here and a story there and never putting it all together. Some people do that. Some of them even give up Christ and the Bible because all they can remember is David and Goliath, and they've forgotten the character of Jesus and the power of the things he said. But if someone claims he's got a message from the Spirit of God, he had better be able to put it in touch with what the whole Bible says. They will never contradict each other; they will support and validate each other.

The Holy Spirit offers us intimacy with God. We are his sons and daughters, and it is the Spirit who assures us of that. Nothing could be more strengthening and helpful than being able to call out to God as a father. But some people take the intimacy farther; they seem not only to believe that God speaks to them, but also that they can speak for God. They feel they've been specially singled out to speak or lead in a completely authoritative way.

Well, there's some indication in Scripture that this is possible. When the Old Testament prophets stood up to speak, they felt they were speaking for God. But there's also plenty of indication that they weren't the only ones claiming it. There were ten false spokesmen for every one who really was dealing with the truth. But the false ones, of course, never got their words written down in the Bible.

So when we're confronted with someone who's claiming to have a pipeline to God, I think we ought to check him out a little. The Bible calls this "testing the spirits."

I recently heard from a girl I've known for some time. She's been through some difficult experiences, and she's emotionally unstable. She's got a problem with alcohol, and she's extremely distraught. Now she's met some young men who are filled with the Spirit and say they are shepherds. Each of them has a little group, eight or ten people, primarily young women, who work and turn their money over to the shepherd. They aren't supposed to do anything without first consulting the shepherd. All this because these young men feel this is something God asked them to do.

Now, really, this is hard to judge. This particular girl, and probably many of the others, really could use the guidance of a good substitute father. But is it a biblical pattern for one person to take over the mind of another adult and control her? I would say no.

I think there are several questions you have to ask about what you hear. First, does it fit with the biblical pattern? Then, does it go against natural law? We're not encouraged to go against gravity by jumping off buildings, no matter how "spiritual" it seems. Is it in line with the experience of other Christians? Do other wise Christians agree that it is the will of God? All these questions should be asked, and particularly asked about an individual who has set himself above everyone else. On the whole, the Spirit is very democratic. He speaks to everyone who knows God, not just through certain highly spiritual people. So someone who sets himself or herself up as having a special message should be carefully examined.

Gifted People

To speak of the Holy Spirit and not talk about the gifts of the Spirit would be a terrific oversight. There is plenty of controversy about the gifts these days, and of course the Bible places fairly heavy emphasis on them.

It's amazing how blind we can be. If you read the parts of the Bible that talk about the gifts—Romans 12, First Corinthians 12, Ephesians 4—you get a clear general picture. It goes like this: God gives every Christian a special ability or set of abilities that can't be explained simply by training or natural talent. Every Christian is *different* and has a unique contribution to make to other Christians. Every Christian's gifts are essential; you can't say any person is unnecessary. God has given each of us a wonderful role to play.

So why is it often true that when people talk about the gifts, they end up talking as though everybody ought to be the same? If the message of the gifts of the Spirit is that every Christian is important and necessary, why do we end up feeling inadequate, as though someone else got a better deal?

If you go to a wedding and the mother of the bride cries while the groom's mother laughs, do you assume that one loves her child and the other doesn't? No. You realize that God has given them different personalities and they respond to the same event in different ways. And why do you think we have four accounts in the Bible of one man's life? Each gospel shows a different reaction to one man. This is the chief lesson of the gifts. One man's view is not enough to get a total picture of Jesus. We needed four. One way of responding to the Holy Spirit is not enough. We need many. One kind of ability and giftedness is not enough for a group of Christians. We need all kinds.

I don't think we necessarily need to look at the lists of gifts mentioned in the Bible and get terrifically detailed about who has which ones. I don't think those lists are meant to be exhaustive. Too often we see the trees and miss the forest. The overall point is that, in the work the Spirit does in our lives, everyone is essential, and everyone is different. We should quit trying to cram each other into molds. The Spirit never does.

Less Than Human

Sometimes you hear people talk about being "led by the Spirit." At times they will go even further and speak of being "Spirit-controlled." That raises another observation I'd like to make on the Holy Spirit. Someone has said it this way: "The Holy Spirit is a gentleman. He will never come into a situation unless you ask him to."

This is in opposition to what some people seem to mean when they talk about being controlled by the Spirit. They seem to have in mind the heavenly side of the familiar statement "the devil made me do it."

There is a powerful temptation to become less than human, to turn off our minds and let feelings push us around, or to let someone else tell us what to do. I don't believe this is ever the work of the Holy Spirit. The emotions are to have full play, but so is the mind. You see, God loves *you*—not your carcass. If he needed a body to push around, he could make another one very quickly. He wants you to develop into the full person you were made to be.

The Spirit is involved in many other areas of our lives —in fact, in every area. He's the interpreter of our prayers; I'm sure that many things we ask for are absolutely impossible, not because they are scientifically impossible, but because they violate the whole scheme God is developing. But the Spirit goes beyond our words and understands what we really want.

It is the Holy Spirit who produces love, joy, peace, patience, and the other Christian virtues in our lives.

It is the Holy Spirit who continually stands, through a person's conscience, for a right way, so that there is never a lack of right to judge wrong by, and so that people are, at some level, conscious of their need for God's forgiveness.

It is the Holy Spirit who impregnates our minds with God's wisdom, so that we can make the right decisions when we have to choose. He even overrules our judgment and points us in another direction when we're off the track.

I could go on and on. There's no limit to what the Holy Spirit does, because there is no limit to the involvement God wants to have in your life. He involves himself with you through the Holy Spirit.

Who's Got the Spirit?

Christians seem to be having some trouble with the Holy Spirit lately, fighting over who has him, who's *really* listening to him, and what you have to do to get him.

I don't think the fighting is at all necessary, except perhaps in some extreme cases. There are three general ways we are involved with God's Spirit, and I think the problem lies in emphasizing one over the others.

First, we receive God's Spirit when we become Christians. There can't be any argument over that; read Romans 8:9. You don't receive a chunk of him with more to come; you can't divide a person into pieces. You receive all of him.

But since it's a beginning relationship, you don't know all there is to know about him. In fact, you probably don't know much at all. So it's natural that, as time goes by, you learn more about him, and more about yourself. That's the second thing the Spirit does—teaches you and helps you grow. It may be that your growth will be gradual, and it may come in big quantum jumps. If you go through a tremendous jump, you'll be tempted to look back and say, "I didn't know anything before." And you'll be tempted to look around at everyone else whose experience is different and consider those people lacking something.

But that would be a terrible mistake. God, remember, is not speaking to the masses through his Spirit; he is speaking to individuals. Each person has his own way of growth, and you can only superficially compare it with others.

The final thing the Spirit does in our lives is perfect us. None of us has seen that yet; we will see that when we see Christ face-to-face and become like him. It's important to remember that this is still to come, because sometimes we get the impression that we've arrived. No way. We may know more of God than we did a year ago, but compared to what there is to know, we know nothing.

We're on the road, and the Holy Spirit is leading us, helping us, comforting us, and speaking to us. To him, each one of us is special, and he treats us as individuals.

TAKEOFF

Think for a minute about your best friend. What do you like about him or her? What makes that person such a good friend? Make a list of things you appreciate about your friend.

Do you think about God as a friend? What do you like about him? Make another list. Compare the list for similarities and differences.

If you were going to explain to a friend what it means to know God personally, what would you say? Write out your answer or use a cassette recorder. Reread or listen to your answer. Then scan the chapter again for help in filling any gaps in your explanation.

---o---

Several passages of Scripture were mentioned in this chapter. But there's another one that gives us a look at Jesus' teaching about how a person enters into a relationship with God as a member of his kingdom family. You can read the account in John 3.

We
don't have to
hide sin
in a moldy
corner.
Chuck Isaacs
Ed Wallowitch

5

Is God Mad at Me?

I was walking toward the pool, my towel over my shoulder, and met Linda. "Hello," I said, and she sank to the ground and started crying.

I had no idea what was going on. I sat down next to her and asked what was wrong, but she didn't answer. So I sucked on a blade of grass for a while, and eventually she turned to me.

"What's wrong?" I asked.

"I'm the worst girl in the world," she said.

"What on earth makes you think that?" I asked, but she began to cry again. Feeling awkward, I searched for something to say. "You know, there's a lot of competition out there. I could believe you're pretty bad, but the worst girl in the world—you'd really have to work at that."

"Don't make fun of me," she said. Then she told me about the past year.

"I was the first sophomore in our school ever to be a varsity cheerleader. I got to go to all the upper-class events and eventually found myself dating a senior, the best basketball player in the school. We went everywhere together. Soon we were going steady.

"Then they had a senior ditch day, and I heard afterwards that my boyfriend had gone with another girl. We had a scene, right in the hall with everyone watching. I threw his ring at him and ran into the washroom and cried. I stayed home from school for two days because I couldn't go and face my friends.

"One evening some girls drove by the house and blew the horn. They weren't the kind of girls I usually hang around with, but I was really low—feeling sorry for myself, and tired of sitting around the house. So I went with them. We drove to a town about twenty miles away and pulled into a drive-in next to some guys. We talked to them and eventually paired off.

"The next day at school there were stories about me all over the place. Kids at my school can be like cannibals. People want to tear you apart, and if you give them any opportunity, they will. The girls told people I'd done things I never had, and everyone believed them. No one would believe me. I said to myself, If that's the kind of girl they think I am, then that's the kind of girl I'm going to be. And for the rest of the year, I've been just that. I'm a mess. I'm the worst girl in the world."

Worse Than Bad?

As I started talking with Linda, I was reminded what a common problem guilt is. Everybody feels it at times—maybe not as strongly as Linda did, but we do feel guilt.

Guilt is more than a feeling, however. It is a reality for all of us. We've all sinned. We are all guilty.

Sometimes we make the mistake Linda made of assuming one sin makes us worse than another, or that a lot of sin is worse than one sin. God doesn't see it that way. He doesn't have a "bad, worse, worst" rating for sins. He is so holy that any sin is abhorrent to him. That means any sin, whatever it is, alienates us from God.

To illustrate this point, I often use the analogy of a fifty-five gallon barrel of clean, white table salt. If there is nothing in the barrel but salt, you have fifty-five gallons of

100 percent pure salt. But how much pepper would you have to add to make that fifty-five gallons of salt impure?

You'd only have to add one tiny flake of pepper. That would be a mixture of 99.9999999999999999999999999 (give or take a few 9's) parts salt and (give or take a few 0's) .00000000000000000000000001 parts pepper. But you'd no longer have pure salt.

God has the same view of sin. He's so perfect, so concerned about purity that one sin makes us impure. So we all qualify as sinners.

Then the issue for people like Linda, you, and me is not what was done (or even how we handle our *feelings* of guilt). The important question is: How do we deal with our real guilt and with the sin that makes us guilty?

Some people rationalize their guilt. They blame what they did on other people or circumstances, and pretty soon they rub out the guilt feelings their conscience gave them.

Others say, "Let your conscience be your guide," but I doubt that's wise. Your conscience is a vary tamable animal. Adolf Eichmann, who helped destroy six million Jews, showed almost no remorse. He said he would jump into his grave with glee, because he believed he hadn't done anything wrong. He'd tamed his conscience.

One favorite way of taming your conscience is what I call the "Harper Valley PTA" mentality. "Harper Valley PTA" was a song quite a few years ago about a woman who's being put down by the PTA members. So she goes to their meeting and tells them how bad *they* are. The implication is, "I'm better than you, because, even though we're all bad, I don't pretend to be better than what I am. At least I'm honest." Well, being honest doesn't count for much if you're just honest about being bad. You're still bad.

But most people don't handle guilt that way. They may excuse themselves, but when you get beneath the surface, they're like Linda. They're really sorry for what they've done.

That's a necessary starting point. I'd rather see someone broken down with grief than arrogantly refusing to admit wrongdoing, like Eichmann.

But just being sorry doesn't necessarily help. It wasn't helping Linda; in fact, it was destroying her.

How Sorry Can You Get?

Skid row bums are sorry. It used to be quite a sport in Chicago to take visitors down to see them. You would roll up the windows, lock the doors, and drive around looking at the bums lying in the doorways and gutters. You told your children, "Don't point at the men," so you drove along looking at them out of the corners of your eyes. You didn't want to embarrass them.

But if you did what the bums wanted, you'd tell your children, "Point at them! Shame them!" Most of them were on skid row to punish themselves. They were sorry for something they'd done, and were ruining their lives to prove how sorry they were. By shaming them you helped them punish themselves.

But skid row sorrow doesn't help. In fact, it destroys. Second Corinthians 7:8–11 tells us that. Paul's first letter had really let the church at Corinth have it, and now he wrote something like, "I'm glad I made you sorry, because it made you repent. Your sorrow was godly sorrow. But there is another kind of sorrow—worldly sorrow. And worldly sorrow leads to death."

The bums on skid row have worldly sorrow. It is remorse—taking upon yourself the responsibility for something you've done wrong and living with it. Nothing will destroy people faster.

You want to see clear examples of worldly and godly sorrow? Look in the Bible. Two of Jesus' disciples are perfect examples: Judas and Peter.

The World's Most Unpopular Man

Judas is without doubt the world's most unpopular man. What father ever looks at his newborn son and says,

"I think I'll name him Judas"? No man in history is so despised.

But this sometimes makes us paint Judas in the wrong way. We think of him as a sneaky, traitorous, dirty little so-and-so who never had any intention of following Jesus in the first place. That's far from what Judas was like. For one thing, he was the treasurer.

You don't take the sneakiest person in the group and make him treasurer. You couldn't tell the disciples from other people on the street by the halos around their heads. You could tell them, however, by the absence of a bulge where a guy normally carries his billfold. Why? Because all the disciples gave their billfolds to Judas. He was chosen to handle the money for the whole group. They trusted him!

And Judas did choose to follow Jesus. I think he was originally sincere in wanting to help Jesus set up a new kingdom. But once a woman was dumping some perfume on Jesus. It wasn't an Evening in Paris, $2.99 concoction. It was expensive—some say the equivalent of five to ten thousand dollars in our day. Well, Judas was incensed. He suggested the money be given to the poor (though John says he wanted the money himself). Jesus rebuked him. He told him they'd have plenty of time to help the poor, but not much time to glorify him before he was gone. It put Judas off, and his faith in Jesus went down from there.

But lots of people missed Jesus' point. Peter did, too, even though he was in the disciples' inner three. He was one of the very few men in history to hear the audible voice of God, when God said, "This is my beloved Son, hear him." But that didn't keep him from making mistakes. He missed the point of Jesus' life so badly once that Jesus said to him, "Get behind me, Satan."

At the time of Jesus' crucifixion, tremendous pressure was put on both these men. Judas had been steadily losing faith in Jesus, and he did the worst thing possible —he betrayed Jesus for thirty pieces of silver. He felt guilty, and after they arrested Jesus he tried to undo it by giving the money back. But the Pharisees wouldn't take it. They laughed at him and made fun. With their laughter ringing in his ears, he threw the money down and ran out of the room. He felt absolutely awful. He thought of James and John and the big fisherman Peter. He'd spent three years with them, and now, how could he ever face them again?

The Big Fisherman Blew It

About the same time Judas was beginning to doubt Jesus, Peter was going through a similar crisis. He had just told Jesus that he would never desert him, and when Jesus was arrested, he had followed behind him even though everyone else had run. Maybe he hoped to rescue him. He waited outside while Jesus was on trial, warming his hands at a fire.

A girl asked him if he were one of Jesus' followers. Peter got scared and swore that he wasn't. It happened twice more that night—he did what he knew was wrong, what he'd sworn never to do—he denied knowing anything at all about Jesus. Suddenly, when he heard the rooster crow, he remembered that Jesus had predicted he'd deny him, just that way. Peter fell apart. Peter, the big, strong fisherman, ran out weeping bitterly.

Judas and Peter had both blown it—and they both were sorry. But how did they respond to their guilt? Judas was determined to demonstrate how sorry he was. Eventually he thought of a plan that would prove it. No one would ever be able to deny he was sorry for betraying Jesus. He went as far as any person can go to prove his regret; he went out and killed himself. The Bible leaves no doubt that Judas is separated from God today. He was sorry, but his sorrow wasn't godly sorrow.

Peter's was. But was he more sincere than Judas? I doubt it. The next time we see him, he's preaching at Pentecost, bringing thousands of people to faith in Jesus. What's the difference?

The difference is in the object of the sorrow. The remorseful man puts all the blame on himself, and keeps it there. He wants it to weigh him down so he and everyone else will know he's sorry. That's what Judas did.

But the repentant man—the man who's sorry in God's way—puts the guilt and the pain on the cross by trusting Jesus' forgiveness. He leaves it there and goes on following Jesus. That's what Peter did.

People in southern Indiana tell a story about a man riding down the road on a donkey, carrying a two-hundred-pound sack of wheat on his shoulders. Another man asked him, "Why don't you take the weight off your own shoulders and put it on the donkey?" The man on the donkey replied, "You don't think I'm going to ask the donkey to carry all that weight, do you?"

I think a lot of people are the same way. They hear Jesus say, "Come to me, all of you who are tired from carrying heavy loads and I will give you rest" (Matt. 11:28 TEV), and they decide to go to him. But they still carry the burden of all the things they're sorry for. They're like people washing up to take a bath. You don't clean up before you take a bath; you take the bath for the purpose of getting clean. It's the same with guilt. You don't clean up your own guilty life through self-sacrifice, self-punishment, and self-destruction so that God can accept you. You go to God first and let him clean things up. Sorrow and self-pity really don't please God at all. In fact, they get in his way. What he wants is godly sorrow that repentantly brings burdens to him and lets him keep them.

From a Bug to a Butterfly

That's the story I told Linda. I told her about Peter and Judas, and when I got done I said, "Would you like to pray?" She did. She said, "God, I'm embarrassed about all these things. I've tried very hard to tell you I'm sorry. I've been doing these things because I felt so bad about myself . . . I've been trying to hurt myself. I know that Jesus died on the cross for my sins. He was destroyed for my sins, and I can't get rid of my sins by destroying myself. So help me, God, to accept that and follow you."

It transformed her. Maybe you've read the story Franz Kafka wrote, *The Metamorphosis*. It tells about a man who woke up one morning, having turned into a bug. This was just the opposite. Linda thought she was a bug, and she turned into a butterfly right before my eyes. Suddenly she looked beautiful, and her whole outlook was different. She'd stopped holding onto that sorrow and let it go. She was ready to follow Jesus.

Your whole life as a Christian will be full of moments like that. God knows you are going to blow it. He was aware of that the moment you first came into his family, but it didn't make him kick you out.

Repentance is a constant relationship with God. You don't have to hide sin in a moldy corner. You don't have to work up to a big, emotional "I'm sorry" scene. You just have to learn to walk in a spirit of repentance, where you're more and more aware of how far short you are of what God wants, but also aware that God will forgive you and will bestow the power to overcome. That's what godly sorrow means. Instead of leading to death, as remorse does, it leads to life—forgiven, free, precious life.

When you and I find that kind of life, we make a marvelous discovery. We finally begin to realize that one of the most incredible characteristics of the God who created the world, who loves us like a father, who sent his Son to show us what he himself was like, is his endlessly generous forgiveness.

Despite the guilt we feel, God is never mad at us. He hates our sin with a passion. But he loves us with a forgiveness that can cover it all.

TAKEOFF

Think about the earliest memory you have of doing something wrong. How did you handle your guilt? Did you respond in one of the ways suggested on page 65?

What about the most recent wrong that you have committed? Did you handle that guilt any differently?

If you were going to be tried in court for all the sins you have committed in your life, what would the charges be? List as many as you can in five minutes, starting with the most recent. If you've already asked God's forgiveness for those sins, tear up your list and take a few minutes to thank him for his grace.

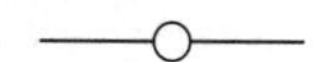

If you want to discover just how much the Bible has to say about this subject, I'd suggest you get a topical Bible or a concordance. Do a study of the words *guilt, sin, forgiveness,* and *grace.* You'll find enough to keep you reading for a long time.

Strix Pix—David Strickler
World Wide Photos

The question crops up when a loved one dies of cancer.

6

Why Does God Allow Such a Messed-up World?

Jimmy was a big guy who played tackle for Redmont High School. One night over coffee he told me about his girl friend. "We've been going together for almost a year, and the whole time I've been praying that she become a Christian. But she hasn't. How come?"

Susan came up to me one night after I spoke. "I can't believe in the God you talk about," she said. "He's trivial. All he cares about is whether people drink and smoke dope. He can't care about the millions of starving people around the world, or else he'd do something for them. He didn't do anything to prevent the slaughter of millions of Cambodians. He didn't even stop Hitler."

Susan's questions sound more serious than Jimmy's. But they are both struggling with the same issue. Sooner or later, most of us end up asking this kind of question. If God really loves people, why doesn't he make them do the right thing? It's a question that has kept a great number of people from believing in a God who is a loving father, who cared enough to send his Son to prove that love.

Why Doesn't He Do Something?

Usually it hits you suddenly. You read *The Diary of Anne Frank,* or a friend is killed in a car wreck caused by a drunk driver, or you see a film on starving children. And you're faced with the question: Why isn't God more involved?

To understand this, I start with three stories Jesus told in Luke 15: the stories of the lost sheep, the lost coin, and the lost youth (better known as the Prodigal Son).

In the sheep story, one sheep is lost. The shepherd leaves all the rest of the sheep behind and searches for it. He finds it, brings it home, and everybody's ecstatic. The same with the lost coin. The woman searches the house until she finds it and puts it in a safe place. But the lost son is different. When he's lost, the father stays home and waits for him to return.

Now, why is it that when a sheep's lost, the shepherd goes after it; when a coin's lost, the woman looks for it; but when a kid's lost, the father stays home? Isn't the boy as valuable as a sheep or a coin? Obviously he is.

Then why doesn't Jesus have the father go after him?

He doesn't go after him because he's applying a principle people know better from their day-to-day living than from their theology: Force doesn't work with human beings. If the father got a big, mean servant to go and drag the kid home, then threw him in the back bedroom and said, "You can come out when you're ready to shape up," the kid would sit on the edge of the bed and say, "You just wait until I get out of this bedroom. I'm going right back where I was. I was ready to make it big in pork. I could have been the Oscar Mayer of the far country. It's just like my dad to interfere, right when I was going to succeed."

The lesson would never be learned. So the father has to wait at home, worried sick, until the kid wakes up. He has to come to that point by himself.

That's the difference between objects and people. A

person has a choice whether to live in harmony with God or not. Sheep and coins do not. If God wants to have a person love him, he won't use coercion. (Remember: Restraint is one of the evidences of a father's love.) God could light up the sky with letters forty miles high and convincingly prove he exists. But that would wipe you out; you'd have no choice but to respond to him.

Imagine a guy who wants to get a girl to love him. Probably the guy is strong enough to overpower the girl. He could, just by brute strength, get the girl to do anything he wanted her to do. But he doesn't. He wants a love relationship. He doesn't want a robot who will do what he wants if he twists her arm enough. He wants her to respond willingly. That can never happen if he takes away her power to resist him. He has to offer himself gently and without force.

Now what does this have to do with the questions that opened this chapter? Just this: God could overpower the world. He could wipe out all the Stalins and the Hitlers. He could prevent every drunk's car from starting. He could take away the excess wealth from people who have more than enough, and redistribute it to poverty-stricken and starving people. God could do all that; but he doesn't. If he did, we'd be so shattered we'd *have* to fall to our knees and worship him. We'd have no choice as to whether to love him or not. It wouldn't be a love relationship; it would be rape. It would ruin the human project.

You see, God has a number of projects. His plant project, animal project, and human project are only part of the bigger earth project. Then there's the planetary project, the solar system project, and on and on. Each project is meant to glorify God. The human project is a little different from the others in that God made human beings to respond voluntarily to what he wants. And man has rejected that. The Bible traces it back to the beginning of time, when the first man and woman rejected God, chose their own way, and made a mess of things.

Now think a little while about what an incredible thing

this is. The whole universe is in harmony with God. It glorifies God by doing in an orderly fashion what it's designed to do. The stars don't just zoom around up there. People predict things by them. Sailors steer ships by them. People tell the exact time by them more accurately than by any ordinary clock.

And it's a huge universe. If you could make a spaceship that would go the speed of light, it would take you only eight minutes to get to the sun from our planet. But you could spend fifty thousand years traveling in our galaxy. To get to the next galaxy would take about a million years. Then if you got bored and wanted to go on to the next galaxy, you'd have to go for some two to six billion years.

This unthinkably huge universe moves in perfect order. It's in complete harmony with what God wants. But over in one corner, one little speck called Earth, one of the smallest of the planets, has these two-legged things that have the right to stand up on their hind legs in the middle of all that order and say, "*I* do what *I* want to do because *I* want to do it, and God had better leave *me* alone." And God listens to them and he will leave them alone.

Take a look at a tree. It's a beautiful thing, tremendously complex. It's part of the rain cycle, part of the oxygen/carbon dioxide cycle. All the tremendously complex and perfect aspects of a tree glorify God, but they do it involuntarily. A tree can't stand there and say, "I will not participate in the carbon dioxide cycle." It has to. A person, however, can say that. He can commit suicide; he can completely disrupt the peaceful world God has in mind for him.

Now why did God give that right? Why, out of all the creatures in the universe, did he give that right to a person to disrupt things? It must be because voluntary cooperation, the love that a person can give God, is incredibly valuable. God lets our planet be a potential blemish in the universe so that humans can choose to be everything they're meant to be by choosing him. It's a tremendously valuable thing to God.

Another "Why?"

We've talked so far about why God lets people make bad choices and even hurt other people. But that's only part of what most people question when they ask, "Why does God allow such a messed-up world?" Another side of the question was raised by Kay, a small, mousy girl who came to talk to me after I spoke to a group of kids about faith.

"I can't believe in God any more," she said as she started to cry. Kay went on to tell me how her little sister had drowned in a flood. How she'd seen her sister's swollen body when they finally found it down river. When she finished the story, Kay asked me, "Why would God let that happen? If he's in control of everything, and if he loves everybody, why did he let Patty die?"

To my thinking, this is a tougher question to answer than "How could God let Hitler kill six million Jews?" The Hitler question is tied directly to the ideas we've talked about already—the human project and the value God places on a person's choice to do right or wrong. But that doesn't explain why natural disasters—floods, tornadoes, earthquakes—destroy people.

I've heard some Christians respond to such questions by arguing that natural disasters show the power of God at work in the world. Or that God triggers tragedies like the flash flood that killed Kay's sister to somehow teach us a valuable lesson about him or about life.

I once faced an example of this kind of thinking at a funeral. A young girl and a friend had fallen off a mountain in an avalanche. Rescue workers didn't find the bodies buried in the snow until many hours too late.

But at this funeral, the minister stood up and said, "Isn't it wonderful how God in his marvelous love has covered these two girls with a blanket of his beautiful white snow?"

I wanted to jump up and scream, "No! That's false!"

Those girls' deaths weren't beautiful. The girls were

crushed and suffocated as they screamed in terror. They died horrible, agonizing deaths, as did Kay's little sister.

If a loving God does that as an act of love, then we have to redefine love.

I've struggled with this kind of thinking all my life. And I've known many others who've shared the same struggle. If God really loves people, how do you explain disasters, disease, and accidents that destroy people in such awful ways?

I don't think there are any easy answers. But after discarding some unacceptable explanations, I've come to a more comfortable conclusion: Believing God is the sovereign creator and in control of the world doesn't mean he is directly, causally connected with everything that happens on this earth. He doesn't make the decision to reach down and shake loose a rock to start every avalanche.

When some people hear this kind of thinking, they get nervous. They feel God's control of the universe is being threatened. They think I'm limiting God. I'm not. But I am saying God doesn't ordinarily interfere with the natural course of the universe any more often than he directly interferes with man's choices.

Perhaps the best way to explain what I mean is to introduce an idea I've found very helpful in hassling through this issue—the idea of conflicting autonomies. The best discussion of conflicting autonomies I could recommend is in Langdon Gilkey's book, *Maker of Heaven and Earth.* But I'll try to explain the idea briefly here.

We've already talked about how God's creation includes various projects—the human project being only one. We've discussed how, when God started the human race, he gave us the ability to choose our own course—right or wrong. In giving us that power, he provided mankind with autonomy. But there were many other autonomies involved in creation.

God set our solar system in motion and gave it autonomy to keep it going. He doesn't have to whack the earth like a giant tetherball to keep it traveling in orbit. He doesn't have to give it an occasional spin on his fingertips to keep it revolving. The whole thing keeps moving because God set its course at the beginning and established lasting laws, such as gravity, to keep it all running without his constant attention.

God created countless other autonomies. Our weather system, geological processes that change and shape our earth, the growth and reproduction of cells, our ecological system, and life itself, are a few examples. And all these autonomous systems continue running because God created them and set them in motion, providing the impetus and the laws to keep them all operating.

Sometimes some of these autonomies come into conflict. The world's pollution problem is an example of the conflicting autonomies of mankind and the world's ecological system. A tidal wave that wipes out all the villagers of a Pacific island is an example of the conflicting autonomies of nature and human beings.

A natural tragedy—whether it's a lightning bolt that kills a telephone lineman or a cancer that has eaten away the life of someone you love—should not be viewed as punishment or a capricious act of God. A much better explanation, one more consistent with everything else we know about God, is the idea of conflicting autonomies. Electricity and cancer cells are part of autonomous systems set in motion at the creation of the world—systems that sometimes come into conflict with human life.

That leaves us with another question: How could a perfect God create conflicting autonomies? Maybe this is where we have to apply that verse, "How great are God's riches! How deep are his wisdom and knowledge! Who can explain his decisions? Who can understand his ways?" (Rom. 11:33 TEV).

Perhaps, just as it's impossible to have a beautiful sculpture without chipping, breaking, and reshaping stone, it's also impossible to have a created world without autonomies that bump and grate against each other in occasional conflict.

Historically Christians have believed there is a mysterious connection between a person's decision to sin and such conflicts as natural disaster and disease. In other words, fallen mankind brought about a fallen world. Maybe if mankind hadn't chosen to alienate himself from God, we might be so in tune with God and his creation we wouldn't have come into conflict with other autonomies.

I don't know how all this fits together. But I do know the idea of conflicting autonomies helps me understand that God isn't sitting up in heaven trying to decide whether to stir up a tornado, an earthquake, or some new kind of disaster to punish the world or teach it a lesson. It also helps me believe I'm not the only one who thinks it's rotten that a little girl drowned in a flood, her head banged against pilings and trees, her lungs searing as she suffocated in water. God thinks it's rotten, too. He weeps! Jesus wept at the death of Lazarus, his friend. He sweat blood thinking about his own death. He thought death was awful.

But he also thought there were worse things. One worse thing would be for his Father to forfeit the chance to have people willingly, voluntarily love him by interfering with their power of choice. He could have asked his Father to make a physical assault on the earth, wiping out death and forcing people to acknowledge him. But he considered our humanness more precious than anything else.

With this in mind, I can help a girl like Kay, whose sister drowned, to understand that God still loves her, and even loves her little sister. He's not punishing her for something by killing her sister, and he's not a savage, hostile God. Kay doesn't have to believe it's great that her sister died, either. Understanding who God is and how he's involved with her should let her see God's unimaginably glorious scheme: the voluntary love relationships between man and his God, the cooperation with God that's more than a plant's—the willing giving of ourselves to God because of who he is.

Of course, we have barely scratched the surface of the questions about God's involvement with mankind. You may have said, "Hey wait a minute," several times as you read. If so, I'd suggest you read the books recommended in Takeoff at the end of this chapter. They dig into the questions in a much deeper fashion than it's possible to do here.

It's for sure there aren't any simple answers. But by asking the questions and digging deep, we learn a lot about God and the way he wants to relate to us. It gets us away from a flippant, easy-answer approach to Jesus, and draws us closer to the real God who made this universe —and us.

What a fantastic thing this is! We have the chance for a love relationship—an intimate, giving friendship—with the God who made the vastness of the galaxies. He respects us as men and women. He will not violate our right to refuse him, yet he stands ready to welcome us into his family.

TAKEOFF

What are the most common questions you've heard people ask about injustice in the world? Which ones have bothered you the most? Does the idea of conflicting autonomies apply to these questions? How or why not?

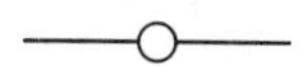

Most of us have a lot of questions relating to the subject of this chapter. Job, in the book of the Bible bearing his name, asks them, too.

Part II

LIVING WITH GOD

Part II

Living with God

I once heard an old wives' tale, or maybe it was a children's story, about creation. According to this tale, when God finished making Adam, he looked him over, then playfully poked him in the stomach and said, "You're done." And that's how people came to have navels. After God creates each one of us, he sticks a finger in our stomach and declares, "You're done."

That's a silly little story. But I've known a lot of Christians who seem to believe in done buttons. Because they come to know God in a personal way, because they understand and believe all the things we've covered so far in this book, they think that God has touched them in a special way and said, "You're done." They plaster some bumper stickers on their cars to declare their faith and figure that's all there is to it.

They're wrong.

Christians should never be "done." Becoming a Christian is the beginning, not the end, of the line. It is absolutely essential to understand, believe, and know God; that's what Part I has covered. But we can't stop here. We have to take what we know and believe and apply it to our lives.

That's what the questions in Part II will cover: Living with God.

Bob Combs
Prayer,
like any other
kind of relating,
takes time
to learn.

7

Does Prayer Change Anything?

One day I drove home from a meeting feeling roughly as though I had been caught in a washing machine. Facing a series of deep and agonizing problems, I felt battered, exhausted, and thoroughly unsettled. The minute I fought free of one problem, another hit me in the face like a wet undershirt. Yet I couldn't stop struggling or I would drown.

Riding home alone, I began to think about what I needed. I decided I only wanted solitude. I wanted time to find myself. I'd have liked to ask somebody to join me, but for the life of me I couldn't think who. I needed a friend closer than a brother, someone who simply wouldn't leave me or give up on me, no matter what. I needed a place where all the complex problems could come into perspective and be sorted out.

And where do I find that kind of place, and that kind of friend? The only place I can find it is with God. He is a friend who will never leave me or forsake me. He knows me intimately. He sees the future, and he knows exactly how my personal dilemmas will work out. He puts everything into perspective; the things I see as overwhelming look fairly trivial from his perspective. Most of all, he loves me. *Loves!*

So what do I do? Do I take out a pencil and paper, make a list of all my problems, and then ask God to solve each one? No, that's not really what I need.

My problems go deeper, and so must their solution. I have a relationship with God himself. And if I think about that relationship strictly as something I profit from, it isn't a relationship.

A guy who claims to love a girl, yet only talks to her to get her in bed, to get some pleasure from her, doesn't know much about relationships or about love. Yet that is exactly how most of us are tempted to talk to God.

An Insensitive God?

Prayer is getting in touch with God on an intimate, personal basis. Shutting your eyes may help; many people find it does. But staring out of a window or taking a walk may help, too. That doesn't make it less prayerful.

We all have misconceptions about prayer we need to get rid of. First, prayer isn't trying to get an insensitive God to be sensitive. We all act as if it were at times, though. "Dear God, I'm terribly concerned about the people in Bangladesh. I really feel their pain. I wanted to point out their situation to you." An old pop song from a few years back put it: "What the world needs now/Is love, sweet love. . . . Lord, if you really want to know." But God doesn't need our instructions in loving. The real God is infinitely sensitive and compassionate.

Nor is prayer trying to help a forgetful God remember. We have the idea that if we get really emotional, or raise our voices, or assume a certain posture or way of holding our hands, or use polysyllabic religious words over and over, God, who is slightly deaf, will hear us and remember the thing he forgot. But God isn't like that.

Finally, prayer is not trying to make an unwilling God willing. That idea sounds like this: God's got all this power saved up, with which he could cure all the leukemia patients in the world just as easily as you flip a lock of hair out of your face. So I'm going to beg him until he'll do it. He's kind of lazy, and he doesn't like to use his power very often, so I've got to keep pulling on him and begging until he heals my father or my grandfather.

There is a place for persistence in prayer, but this nagging goes beyond persistence. It assumes an unwilling God you can bully into something.

All these kinds of prayer are disqualified because they don't match up with what we know is true of the God we've talked about in Part I of this book. He is absolutely loving, absolutely concerned.

Baseball and Bangladesh

In order to find out what prayer really should be, we need to think first about what I label "larger concerns." Suppose I want to play a baseball game, and I'd rather not have to play it in the rain. So I get together with a group of my friends and pray that it doesn't rain.

However, twenty miles away there is a farmer whose family and livelihood depend on corn growing, and corn has to have rain. In fact, the whole cereal crop for the entire world depends on the right amount of rain. Yet I think I can jump in and twist God's arm to let me play my game.

And actually, God's concerns are even larger than that. He is concerned about people starving. But, as we discussed in chapter 4, apparently there are things even more significant than that—things like the way God comes into a human heart humbly and without force.

God could wave his hand and feed the whole world, or send rain clouds scattering so I can play my game. But he wants us to see him as more than a big miracle machine. He normally feeds the earth through indirect means like farmers, instead of personally and miraculously. He doesn't want to dazzle us; he wants us to love him voluntarily. It's a larger concern I doubt any of us would even think of when we pray. Yet God holds it constantly in mind. I think about my baseball game; he's concerned about people in India and about the whole way he's working in history.

James 4:3 says the reason we don't get what we ask for is because we ask with the wrong motives—"you want only what will give *you* pleasure." If my prayers are narrow, concerned only with myself and not with the larger concerns of the world, God isn't going to respond to them. God's vision extends beyond my horizons.

Another facet of prayer I find important to think about is what I call the "flip side" of prayer. I know the result I'm looking for when I pray, but is there an unseen side? If all my prayers were answered just the way I prayed them, what would be the result? Is the result something that is in line with God's overall plan?

Suppose a tornado is roaring across a field toward my house. I pray, "God, protect me. Wipe out my neighbor's house if you have to, but supernaturally intervene to protect me and my house." If God answers me and the tornado hops over my house, or takes a sudden detour and goes around my property line, I'd no doubt be grateful to him. (Though if the tornado detoured through my neighbor's property, he might not be as thrilled as I.)

But suppose that kind of prayer were answered every time I got into trouble. Suppose whenever I went into a skid on an icy road, I could pray for help and the laws of physics and chemistry would be violated, making my tires supernaturally grip the road. And every time there's a natural disaster, I would get out of it. Every time I would start getting sick, I would pray and suddenly I would be well again. My friends, too, would seem to have miraculous cures from cancer and other diseases.

Those are nice things, but is there a flip side? I think there is. After a while, I think, my neighbors would start muttering to themselves. They might want to get on my good side so they wouldn't get cancer. But on the other hand, they'd wonder about me. I'd be a little inhuman to them.

Now suppose all Christians learned to pray the way I did, so that everything we asked for we got. Soon the Christians would be the people nothing bad ever happened to. Other people would die of starvation, but Christians wouldn't. Other people would have tragedies in their family, but Christians wouldn't. I suspect that if that happened, Christians wouldn't be terribly popular. We'd be a separate race, a race that does not have to live under the natural laws that govern the hostility of our planet. People who lacked our advantage would resent us.

And it would go in diametric opposition to God's plan. The reason Jesus came to earth was to join the human race, not escape it. As his followers, we too are to share the hurts and sorrows of other people. Jesus did work miracles to remove some of those hurts, and he does today. But miracles are always exceptions. If they were everyday, normal occurrences, we wouldn't call them miracles.

Exceptions aside, Jesus didn't invite us all to leave the real world and join some Magic Kingdom where there are no problems. His idea was that, facing the world just as other people face it, we'd learn to transcend or transform those problems with his power.

Jesus said we are the salt of the earth. If salt doesn't get mixed in with the food it's supposed to season, it is useless. We too are supposed to mix up with all the confusion and problems of the human race and transform them through God's presence in us. But if we could make God turn us into a plastic-sealed, problem-proof race, we'd have lost all our ability to communicate the message Jesus brought to the world.

The "I'm special" mentality is repulsive to people. If it is always possible for me to coerce God into healing a friend of mine from leukemia, then the question has got to be raised, Why in the world can't I get God concerned enough to heal the whole cancer ward? He doesn't come down to heal the whole hospital, so he must be either a God who plays favorites, or a God who has limited power—he can do only one zap a day, and he's already used it on me.

Not only would that mentality alienate you from your neighbors, but it would eventually make your relationship with God flippant. Prayer would be something you use to control God, like magic. It'd be a plaything. God would become a machine. You'd have to punch all the buttons in the right combinations to make him work.

So when I pray, I need to think about the flip side of prayer. What happens if I really get my way with God, not just this time, but every time?

A Junior Merlin

Actually, I don't think the primary purpose of prayer is getting God to do things at all. I believe that prayer is the process of getting to know God. It isn't God who changes when I pray; it's me. I get my knowledge, my desires, my will, and my thoughts in tune with his, so that we really become one. Gradually I find that I want the same things God wants for this world, and I'm willing to allow him to use me to bring about those things.

Now most people really aren't interested in that kind of prayer. They're not terribly interested in changing themselves or getting to know God. They'd rather have a magic show. They are interested in being junior Merlins. All they see in the Bible is miracles; it's a kind of Ripley's *Believe It or Not.* They want to be able to decide things for God, like who should live or die, who should be healed, who shouldn't, whose farm should be destroyed, whose baseball game should be rained out, whose football team should win, which heavyweight champion should knock out the brains of the other. You can tell that's what they want out of prayer, because the more they get their way with God, the better they like praying. They enjoy the power. Essentially, they would rather be God themselves than allow God to be God.

But being a junior Merlin is not ultimately satisfying. There is a basic human desire to control things, but it isn't the most basic. The most basic need is to know God, to let his personality and his presence fill your life. It's a hunger so deep, so gnawing, that if you let it come to the surface of your life it can almost overcome you. Mostly we keep it hidden, even from ourselves. But I suspect every one of us wants to know God on an intimate level, and wants it far more than any other thing we've ever prayed for.

Many people seem to think that becoming a Christian means automatically having that deep, intimate level of peace with God. Actually, asking Jesus Christ to enter your life is more like an introduction. When you're introduced to someone, you may go away with goose pimples of excitement, or you may feel "So what?" But regardless of your feelings, you don't "know" that person—not yet, anyway. The same with Christ. If you've accepted him into your life, you've got the introduction, but there is a lot of growing to go in your relationship.

Prayer moves you closer to God. I find that thought more exciting than a strictly functional approach to prayer. With a functional approach, you have a washer to wash your clothes, a dryer to dry your clothes, a refrigerator to keep your food cold, aspirin to cure your headache, and God to take care of any problems you can't solve with one of the preceeding things. God goes around finding parking places, keeping your parents from being mad at you, bringing instant recall on tests so that while other kids in your class are rewarded for preparation, memory, and ability, you can come in without preparation, pray a simple prayer, and hit the top of the curve. That's what a lot of people want, but it's not something deeply worthwhile.

Miracles

Now of course God does sometimes intervene in history, and there are miracles. I have seen some, and even if I hadn't, I would only have to read the New Testament to know they exist. We are told to pray for the sick and to ask God for the things we really need. That is a long way, however, from thinking that every time I close my eyes and talk to God about something it should work out just the way I want it to. Instead, at the same time I am talking to God about something, I should be trying to understand what he wants in that situation. I should be trying to align myself with what he wants.

When I pray, I say, "This is what I want, Lord, and what seems best to me. But I know I'm limited. You do what's right and I'll be happy. Thy will be done."

There are some Christians who would say that's wrong. They think I'm giving God a back door out—that I'm showing a lack of faith. I respect them as Christians, but I believe they're wrong about this. I don't think God wants or needs a back door out. I do, however. I want to be able to talk sincerely and frankly to God, telling him just how I feel about situations I care about. Yet I want to let him run the show. I don't want to put up a nonnegotiable demand that isn't the very best thing from his all-seeing, all-knowing point of view.

Do I pray for people? Of course I do. The Bible tells us to. But I don't see praying for people as straightening out God as to what they need. I see it as agonizing beside God over a fellow human being who is in pain. I happen to believe that God sits on the edge of every sick bed in the world, wanting to move in and cure that person. When I pray, I sit beside him, agonizing with him. Often he does heal; most sick people in our society do get well, often with the help of doctors whose wisdom and ability ultimately come from God.

But there are many times when God does not intervene, and when the laws of the universe which he created take their course. That doesn't happen because God likes pain and death. It doesn't happen because no one has come up with the right prayer, and so God can't do anything. It happens because there are more important things in God's view of the universe than whether that person recovers to live another ten or twenty years to die of some other disease. The overarching scheme of God's plan is to work through the human heart, not through flashy miracles.

Some will object, "Doesn't your kind of prayer leave out faith?" But it seems to me the facts are the other way around. Is faith in the strength and fervor and "rightness" of my prayers? Then it's in something that doesn't really deserve the absolute confidence of faith—me. I know myself well enough to question my motives and my ideas about the world. Faith is faith in God, or it isn't faith at all. It is faith that God knows what he is doing, and that he is taking care of us, no matter how desperate things seem to be.

An Anti-Flu Prayer

It's not that prayer lacks benefits.

There are tremendous benefits to letting yourself just be with God in your prayers—to think his thoughts, and listen to his words, and tell him your own feelings, and hold up people and situations to him when you know they need his help. There is tremendous peace that comes from the sense of oneness with God. There is tremendous excitement knowing that you are cooperating with God's will, and your life is going to mean something because you're tied up with God's goals.

When you meet God in prayer, you are meeting someone who loves you in a far greater sense than any boy friend or girl friend ever will. That, not what you can get out of it, should be your motivation in going to him.

Naturally, the greed motive is going to slip in. Just a few weeks ago I had a very bad case of the flu. As I hung my head over the edge of the toilet I was crying out to God to help me stop throwing up. I don't think God minds that, though it is somewhat selfish. Now that I'm well, I'm not praying for other people who are throwing up. He understands my weaknesses. And he wants to hear me expressing my deepest thoughts.

But he also wants me to grow. That's why, at the very same time I was crying to God, I was also saying, "If there's value in this, or something I need to learn, I'm willing to be sick." And I did realize that there might be value just in being sick exactly the way other human beings are. I'm human, and I understand human weakness because I experience it. My neighbor can't say, "Well, Jay has an anti-flu prayer; nothing bad ever happens to him. The minute he gets sick he just sends up this prayer that makes him well. So Jay could never really understand me and my doubts and frustrations, because he doesn't have any."

Beggars Make Poor Friends

So far, we've been discussing prayer as if it was just an asking exercise—a procedure for placing orders with God. Too often that's the only way we think of it. But if prayer is going to be the communication process we use to develop a relationship with God, it needs to be more than a verbal shopping list of desires we send out to some great delivery service in the sky.

Think about your best friend. What kind of a relationship would you have right now if your only conversation with that person was to ask for something? That's no way to build a friendship.

Talking with God must include more, too.

Prayer, like any conversation between friends, ought to include a variety of elements. I don't know where this idea came from, but a friend of mine shared an acrostic with me, A-C-T-S, that has helped me remember the essential elements of prayer.

A–Adoration. I love and adore God for a lot of reasons. I marvel at the incredible beauty I see in his creation and the consistency he has built into the world and its laws. I appreciate his character—his fatherliness, his forgiveness, his willingness to sacrifice his Son, his approachability. I compliment God for those traits by praising him for them as part of my prayer.

C–Confession. If I want a free and open relationship with God, I need to keep the air clean between us. I have to apologize for the mistakes I've made—both deliberate and unintentional.

T–Thanksgiving. Only an ingrate doesn't thank a friend for a gift. And there are so many gifts for which to thank God. I think it's important to sometimes hunt for commonly overlooked gifts to thank God for. The ability to read this book. The incredible variety of colors God created. Our sense of smell.

An attitude of thankfulness—for big things and small—is the best cure I know for depression and discouragement.

S–Supplication. Here's where the asking comes in. We've talked about the asking first in this chapter. But it really belongs here—after the other elements. Supplication is only a part of prayer. The other three parts—adoration, confession, and thanksgiving—ought to be found in every conversation with God.

Prayer, like any other kind of relating, takes time to learn. If you're getting to know a member of the opposite sex, conversation often starts out pretty awkwardly. Then too, after you've known that person for a while, the initial excitement tends to wear off. Talking gets boring. Only when you've known someone for a long time is conversation effortless and relaxed. Relating to God is exactly the same. It can be awkward at first, and the initial excitement does tend to wear off.

The only prescription that works for everybody is persistence. It works in human relationships. If you spend time regularly together, talking honestly or doing things, you're going to develop a deep sense of unity. The same with God. It's often hard to talk to him. You feel as though you're wasting time; you get nervous; you get bored and your concentration on what you're saying (or what he's saying) flees. It's natural, so don't be upset when it comes. But don't give up.

I'd say the first grade in the school of prayer is setting aside one special time for talking to God and doing some inspirational reading, either in the Bible or some other Christian book. Many people find it's best to do it the first thing in the morning; others function better in the evening. Sometimes a study hall, if you can get some privacy, is the ideal time. The only really essential ingredient is quiet, and if you have to take a walk to find it, that's fine.

The graduate school of prayer is, I believe, "prayer without ceasing"—that is, constant prayer as the day goes on. I don't mention this to make you give up on the idea of one time set aside for God—you have to go through elementary school to get to graduate school. But you can begin to take some graduate courses while you're in the lower grades. Try, as your day goes on, to be aware of God. Try to remember his presence when you're faced with a problem, or when you feel angry or worthless. When you feel good, remember to thank him. Treat him as a friend walking by your side.

Does prayer change anything?

Yes. And most of all, it changes you as it brings you closer to the God who is really worth knowing. He is not a push-button God. He is not a God you are trying to get on your side. You are trying to learn to be on his side. You are trying to learn to adopt his principles, his ideas, his understanding and knowledge. Prayer is one of the primary ways to grow to know him.

TAKEOFF

Take a personal prayer inventory. Think back over the past week and make a list of the times you remember praying. What did you pray about each time? Try to make your inventory as complete as possible.

Compare your inventory with this chapter. Put a check mark beside each prayer where your chief purpose was to ask God for something. Are there any others left? Did any of your prayers fit the A-C-T-S pattern?

Make this coming week an experimental prayer period. Go back through the chapter quickly and underline points you think you need to work on. If you have a hard time for a while getting into the A-C-T-S pattern, divide some prayer times into four parts—for four separate prayers. That could force you to work at the parts that come hardest for you.

Next week take another inventory and check your progress again.

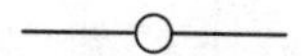

You can read about Jesus' teaching on prayer in Matthew 6:5–18. And if you want some examples of different types of prayer, read a number of David's psalms; you may even want to assign them to one of the A-C-T-S categories.

Even sports can be a spiritual exercise.

Roger Neal

8

What Does It Mean to Be Spiritual?

After I was finished speaking, he came up to me with a look of sublime certainty in his eye. He didn't think I was very spiritual. I hadn't talked enough about prayer, Bible reading, fellowship, witnessing, and other spiritual matters. He was hoping to straighten me out.

So I said, "Will you pray for me?" and I bowed my head. He was taken aback, but he did pray, and I thanked him. Then I began to prove him on his idea of spirituality. Soon it was obvious that my idea of spirituality was a little different from his. I was asking, "Besides praying that the Holy Spirit will bless us by giving warm feelings and cozy groups to share in, isn't it spiritual to pray that he'll show us down-and-out people we can help? Is there a widow on your block whose lawn you could mow? Are there lonely people at school you could be a friend to? Does your church have missionaries overseas whom you could concentrate on praying for? Are you using your money to help anybody?"

And he hadn't really thought of those as "spiritual things."

Just what does it mean to be spiritual? The first definition that comes to mind might be something like "Being in touch with God." But how do you measure that? By good feelings? By the number of people you've witnessed to? How does a person go about being "in touch with God"?

One very popular definition today seems to be "The more removed from the world you are and the more your mind is constantly on spiritual things, the more spiritual you are." Translated into the way other people see Christians, it means, "The more weird you are, the better Christian you must be." It's this kind of definition that brought the sentence "He's so heavenly minded he's no earthly good."

This sort of spirituality only cares about souls. It makes the earth just one big train station: a place where people decide whether they'll get on the train bound for heaven or not; a place to be escaped as soon as possible. You shouldn't use your mind; that's no use to God. The only thing you should read is the Bible. There's a commune in California where they practice this; only the leader can read anything besides the Bible. He reads the newspaper each day so he can report to the group on what Bible prophecies were fulfilled.

Sports, of course, are pointless. So are art, beauty, ecology, politics, you name it. Why should we pay attention to them? The whole point of life is to get off the earth, away from these minds that hang us up with constant questions and doubts, away from these bodies that are always making us lustful or sleepy when we're praying.

Most Christians go through a stage where they believe this. I did. It's popular because most of us don't like life too well. The world is a confusing, demanding, difficult place to live in. It's hostile. We want to put signs on it that read "Danger, Keep Away."

Was Jesus Spiritual?

But when you read the Bible, you have a hard time holding that view. Jesus was criticized for going to too many parties with the wrong kind of people. When he prayed his last prayer for the disciples in John 17, he specifically said, "I do not ask you to take them out of the world."

And if the world is just something we're trying to get away from, why did God look at it after he'd made it and say, "It is very good"?

Besides that, I don't think God is inefficient. If all he cared about were our souls, it'd be much simpler to make us into fuzzy gray balls floating in space. No minds, no real bodies, no personalities—just "souls." Why go to the trouble of making us so complicated?

True spirituality is bigger than just souls, praying, and Bible reading. But how can we define it?

The definition of spirituality I support came to me years ago when I was asking a different kind of question. That was in the early days of Youth for Christ; and some of us in the organization were trying to decide YFC's emphasis.

What hit us then was the fact that people between the ages of thirteen and nineteen are in a very special position. They're adults in many ways, and yet they're still living under other people's authority—their parents, teachers, coaches, and bosses. What does the Bible have to say to their situation?

Really, it doesn't say much. Mostly it deals with men and women who are fully adults. Then we noticed this statement in Luke 2:52 (NIV) about Jesus' boyhood: "And Jesus grew in wisdom and stature, and in favor with God and men."

That statement contains everything we know about Jesus between the time he turned twelve and his baptism at the age of thirty by John the Baptist. Considering the kind of person Jesus turned out to be, those years of development must have been on target. Maybe, we thought, this would give some clues to a young person's spirituality.

So we looked more carefully at that verse to see the various components. First, we noticed Jesus grew in wisdom—that's the sphere of the mind. He also grew in stature—in other words, his body was growing. He grew in favor with God—the spiritual dimension was well adjusted. He got along with his peers.

We looked at those four areas—mental, physical, spiritual, and social—and saw that all of them were important. It wasn't enough to grow only in relationship to God—you also had to grow in relationship to your friends. You had to grow physically and mentally. Why? Because Jesus did.

Later I noticed a similarity in another crucial passage, Romans 12:1–2. Paul writes, "I beg you, my brothers, as an act of intelligent worship, to give him your bodies [physical], as a living sacrifice, consecrated to him and acceptable by him. Don't let the world around you squeeze you into its own mold [social], but let God remake you so that your whole attitude is changed [mental]. Thus you will prove in practice that the will of God is good [spiritual]" (Phillips). Once again, there were four general areas that seemed important.

From this came the concept of the balanced life. Remembering these four areas, we said, helps you keep a healthy perspective on yourself. Everyone will probably emphasize one of these areas more than the others. An athlete will emphasize the physical; a genius will emphasize the mental. But if you remember that all of these areas should show development, then you will be a balanced, healthy person. That's why we still refer today in *Campus Life* magazine and Campus Life Clubs to the "balanced life." We don't think any of these areas should be left out.

True Spirituality

So far, I've mentioned the spiritual as though it were one-fourth of a balanced life, sort of a separate holy little room in your insides.

But that isn't an accurate picture either.

The real truth is more startling, more removed from the

stereotyped "religious" answer. The "spiritual" dimension is the point at which all the other dimensions of life—the mental, physical, and social—are committed to God. There is no spiritual dimension to life where there isn't a mental, physical, or social dimension. Spirituality doesn't happen in a vacuum.

This is where commitment takes on real meaning. When someone becomes a Christian, we say he "commits himself to Christ." But what does that mean? Does it imply a little ceremony in church where you stand up and walk down the aisle? Does it imply only that you pray certain words?

No, it means we commit each area of life to God. God wants us, Paul says in Romans 12, to present our bodies as a living sacrifice to him. The emphasis is on the living. He isn't interested in human sacrifice, as so many pagan religions have thought. He wants living sacrifices: people who eat, play, talk, think, and make friends in a way that is consciously committed to God. That's true spirituality.

The devil also wants a living sacrifice. He wants you to be irresponsible in the way you act. He wants you to eat, play, talk, think, and make friends his way. So there is a constant battle going on over you. And you're the one who makes the decisions.

God wants you to commit your body to him. That means, first of all, that you shouldn't abuse your body. Smoking is a lousy idea. Being out of shape is a bad idea. Drugs and drunkenness are bad ideas. Why? Because they're not responsible uses of your body. They're not wrong because God drew up an arbitrary list of things he wanted to deprive us of. They're wrong because they're against the positive act of committing your body to Christ.

Do you realize sports can be a spiritual exercise? It can be, because God is interested in your body. Are you staying in shape? Do you get enough sleep, eat the right food, keep your weight down? Those are spiritual battles. The devil wants you to be irresponsible. God wants you to be responsible!

It goes further than that. You can misuse your body subtly. A girl can use her body irresponsibly with guys. She can use it to manipulate them. But that's not a responsible use of the girl's body.

A fellow can get infatuated with his body, also. He can care for nothing except how tremendous an athlete he is. He can groom his body as though there were no tomorrow. But that would be irresponsible, too—not because being a good athlete is wrong, but because God made us more than bodies. Athletics isn't an end in itself.

How about your mind? I'd say the biggest lack of spirituality in the realm of the mind stems from laziness. People don't use their minds fully. For some reason Christians are often more guilty of this than other people, as though being ignorant were somehow spiritual. I look around a room of Christian kids and I wonder, "Could there be a cure for cancer in this room? Could there be a great piece of music? Could there be a novel as great as *War and Peace?*"

But it won't happen if you don't give your mind to God. Where do you think Jonas Salk, who discovered the vaccine for polio, would be if he had the typical attitude about chemistry?

And what are you letting your mind soak up? Is it soaking up a lot of quiz shows, or pornography? Or is it becoming saturated with the Word of God?

There are whole other areas of the mind to give to God. How about your thoughts of the opposite sex? Do you think of people selfishly, in terms of what they have to offer you? Or do your thoughts center on how you can responsibly show love to them?

Of course, this spills over into the whole area of relationships. These need to be given to God, too. You should commit your friendships to the kind of relationship that can really reflect God's love. And you shouldn't only include the beautiful people in your friendships. All people are God's children, whether they're lovely to look at or not.

But this social area can be subtle, too. Suppose you have a close group of friends. You value the fact that these friends think highly of you. You value the closeness.

Then suppose someone new starts hanging around the fringe of the group. How do you react? If you're irresponsible, you start thinking how you can protect your status and position in the group. You worry about losing the closeness of your little group. But if you commit your social life to God, then you welcome this person. You trust God to take care of your need for friendship. You look for opportunities to befriend anyone.

These kinds of commitments—physical, mental, and social—go on and on. There isn't any end. The more you experience life and grow as a Christian, the more you find areas of life you need to give to God. Things you wouldn't have thought had anything to do with God become great areas to grow in spiritually.

Suppose you reach eighty or ninety years of age. By this time you've given just about everything in your life to God. There are very few things your commitment to Christ doesn't cover.

Imagine old Fred, eighty-five, riding along in his car with his wife Maude. In front of him there are two teenagers snuggled up to one another. The girl is nibbling the guy's ear and he's got his arm around her. Old Fred gets all worked up. He turns to his wife Maude and says, "Maude, just look at those disgusting kids. Kids just aren't like we were. They have smutty minds. Why aren't they interested in doing things like we did when we were young, like going to church every night of the week, listening to two-hour sermons, and praying for three hours at a time? It's disgusting!"

But Maude leans over and says kind of sweetly, "Fred, remember when we were going together that time we parked out by the cemetery . . . ?"

"I don't remember anything of the kind!" Fred exclaims, and he drives grumpily along muttering about how the kids are going to the dogs.

That night old Fred doesn't sleep too well, and he lies in bed thinking about those kids, and he realizes he was wrong. So he prays, "God, I'm sorry I judged those kids. Help me to mind my own business and to have an open mind about things." Then he turns over and goes to sleep. It's really beautiful, because Fred, at eighty-five, has found yet another area of life he can give to God.

This is spirituality: a living sacrifice to God. It's life committed to God. It's life aware that God is involved, that he is offering his grace and forgiveness.

And it keeps going and growing. That narrow box of "spirituality" divorced from everything else soon becomes irrelevant, just a habit or an emotional release you use occasionally. But real spirituality goes on forever.

TAKEOFF

Get out a sheet of paper. Look up Luke 2:52 and write the verse across the page. Make four columns and title them *intellectual, physical, social,* and *spiritual*—the four parts of the balanced life modeled in that verse.

In each column, list the most significant things you regularly do to grow and improve yourself in that area. When you finish, check yourself out for balance.

Then make four new columns with the same headings and list some goals for growth in that area in the coming month. Double-check yourself by asking, "Are these goals that God would approve of—goals that would help me be a more well-balanced Christian?"

Keep your list of goals for occasional reference. Regularly take time in your prayers to ask God to help you integrate your spiritual life into the other three areas.

———O———

In Matthew 5:3–16, Jesus gave a pretty clear picture of his understanding of spirituality. Galatians 5:22–26 offers some additional characteristics we should exhibit in our lives as Christians.

Temptation strikes in very ordinary ways— through our bodies, our minds, our personalities, our relationships.

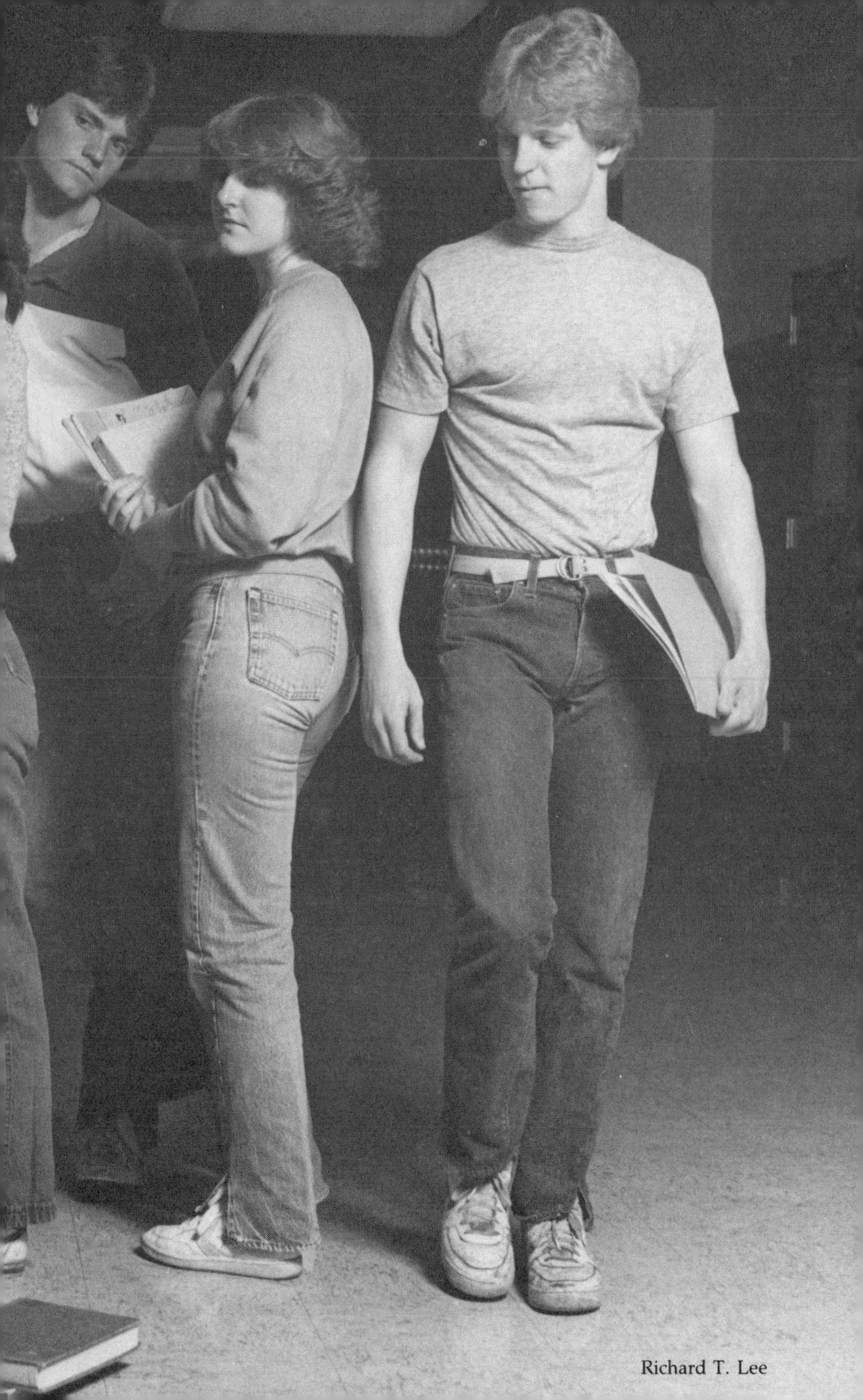

Richard T. Lee

9

Can I Survive in a Non-Christian World?

It was dark. All the meetings were over, and I was walking past the camp dining hall. A huge pile of firewood was stacked beside it, lumpy, dark, and ominous. From behind it came a hoarse, whispering voice.

"Hey, Jay."

I peered into the darkness and made out the figure of a boy I'd seen a lot of that week.

"C'mere a minute," he said.

His name was Neal, about seventeen years old, built like a Greek god. He'd won everything that week—softball, basketball, swimming. He was a fantastic athlete, and seemed to have his head on straight, too. He sat in the front row at every meeting, answered all the questions, volunteered for everything. All the girls thought he was great.

"What's the matter?" I asked, standing with him behind the woodpile.

"I'm worried about what happens when I go home from camp tomorrow," he said.

"What for?" I asked.

"Well, I've been through this before," he said. "Within

the week I'll be acting just like I was before—it happens every year. When I'm up here with Christian kids, I completely absorb their way of life. I know all the songs, I know all about the Bible, I act like they do. And it's not a put-on either, Jay. I really enjoy myself. But at home with my buddies, it's different. I do just as good a job absorbing their environment as I do with Christian kids. I talk bad; I booze it up; I chase after girls—just the opposite of how I am here."

He was staring down at his feet as he was talking. "In fact, Jay, the best way to understand me is this: I'm a chameleon. Whatever color you put me down on, that's the color I turn. I have no character of my own. I just pick up whatever I'm around."

I thought about chameleons. In the third grade, chameleons were the big thing in South Bend, Indiana. There was a five-and-dime store near our house, and in the back they had a pet section with fish, turtles, hamsters, mice, and chameleons. On the way to school we'd buy a chameleon. They'd put it in an ice cream container for us to carry, and when we got outside we'd stuff it in our pockets. If anyone asked us why we had it, we said, "Science."

When things got dull at school, we'd take out our chameleons. They were fun to play with. You could always scare the girls with them. But the neatest thing was watching them change color. For some reason, if you put the chameleon on a book, it would change its color to the book's. Put it half on the geography book and half on the math book, and it'd be half green and half brown.

It seemed great to be a chameleon—you could be any color you wanted. But from the chameleon's point of view, it wasn't necessarily so great. If a chameleon decided he wanted to be gray, and then somebody put him on a green book, he turned green—whether he wanted to or not. He was trapped by his environment, and it could be frustrating to him.

While I was thinking about this, Neal was waiting to

hear what I would say. "Look, Neal," I said, "I think you need to have some real freedom in your life."

"Freedom?" he said. "I've got too much freedom—so much freedom, all I ever do is get into trouble."

"But real freedom isn't the lack of external controls," I said. "Real freedom is being able to choose your own response to any situation. If you're with people who are laughing and you're a free person, you should be able to be sober if you want to. If you're with gossiping people, you should be able to keep quiet if you want. You ought to be able to choose what you want to be, not merely absorb your environment."

I began to tell him the difference between how God and Satan treat you. Read Romans 12, and you'll see their goals. Satan wants to make you conform to the world. He wants you amoebic and shapeless, so that you're not really a person, but merely a result of the environmental influences on you—the people you know, your glands, all the pressures of your surroundings. God, on the other hand, doesn't want you blown by whatever wind comes up—he wants you conformed to the image of Jesus. He wants to shape you from within. That's why we invite Christ *into* our lives. We use that terminology to stress that Christ works on the *inside* before the outside. First John 4:4 says, "Greater is he who is in you, than he that is in the world" (KJV). While Satan is exerting pressure from the outside, through your environment, God is exerting equal pressure inside to help you keep in shape and form.

To illustrate my point, I told Neal a story.

"A few years back the United States had a submarine called the *Thresher,*" I said. "It was lost in the Atlantic. When they finally discovered the wreckage, you know what they found? Some of the bulkheads hadn't been properly welded, and when the ship got down to a certain depth they gave way. The men inside were cooked as if in a pressure cooker. They say sea water came in as live steam. They found only small pieces of the *Thresher,* because the outside pressure was so great that, without a corresponding pressure from the inside, it was crumpled like a piece of paper."

That really got to Neal. "That's me," he said, shaking his head slowly. "But how can I keep the outside pressures from crumpling me?"

"You'll have to understand the difference between being transformed and conformed," I said. "Here in camp you're conforming to a Christian environment; at home you conform to a non-Christian environment. The real issue in Christianity isn't being conformed, but being transformed. Christ didn't come into the world to take you out of the pressure situation. He came to get inside your life and give you inner strength to face it. It'd be worthless to spend all your time at this camp, singing the songs, praying, and fellowshiping with neat Christians. God doesn't want that. That's just another kind of conformity—conformity to a Christian environment. Jesus wants to change you inside, to make you a Christian in more than appearance."

Neal thought about that for a while. "Jay," he said, "I don't think I'm really a Christian." He'd been to camp; he knew all about the Bible; he could act just like a Christian—but he'd never truly accepted Christ. That night he did. The next day he left camp, knowing he didn't have to be a chameleon any more.

Temptation

Often people ask me, "Okay, but what happens next? I've asked Christ into my life, but I still feel pressures outside. How come?"

To start with, there is a great deal of difference between those pressures, which we call temptation, and sin. Some Christians wish they were never tempted. They can't take the pressure, and they say, "I want to be taken out of this." Then they became a hothouse plant. They continually search for little groups that are all Christian—they sing the latest Christian songs, read the latest Christian books, and have great fellowship—but they're useless, because in trying to escape all temptation they've given up their chance to help others.

That's not God's plan. We're all tempted. James 1:12 (KJV) says, "Blessed is the man that endures temptation . . . for he shall receive the crown of life." Apparently if you're not tempted, you don't stand a chance to win the crown of life.

Now what happens when you're tempted? Does Satan come under the door like a mysterious green fog? No. He tries to get you in very ordinary ways—through your body, your mind, your personality, through relationships. He is trying all the time, and there's no way to escape it. God doesn't want you to escape it—he wants you to learn how to handle it.

Take the guy who knows he's a Christian, and knows that he's given himself to the Lord. He goes with his buddies down to the pool and Suzie walks by. Wham! He learns something new about himself. He learns that Christian eyes, dissected by a biologist, are exactly like anyone else's eyes. He thought that once he became a Christian he wouldn't see girls the same way. He thought he'd never notice their pretty bodies. And now he wants to say, "What's wrong? I thought I was a Christian."

But nothing's wrong. Not yet. At this point he has a chance to react as a Christian should, and grow as a Christian. It's an opportunity and a danger. There are two voices he can listen to—the voice of temptation or the voice of the Spirit of Christ, who is inside him if he's a Christian. If he responds irresponsibly and resists the Spirit of Christ, he takes the image of Suzie and puts it in some moist, warm, corner of his life where he fondles it, pets it, and keeps it for future reference.

But there is an alternative. He can say, "Thank you, Lord, for creating Suzie. She's beautiful, and I appreciate that, but I want to look on her as a person, not an object. I want to know her as a total person, with feelings, pain, aspirations."

If a guy reacts that way, he grows as a Christian. He

makes a step he might never have made unless he had seen Suzie. He gives a new part of himself to God. It works a lot better than repressing the whole thing. Saying "I will not think about girls" is about as effective as saying "I will not think about a ten-foot-tall pink elephant." If you say you won't think about it, that's all you'll think of. But if you acknowledge it, and give it to Christ, you can grow in grace through overcoming a temptation.

Too Late

At a Campus Life camp in Colorado, I told about my behind-the-woodpile conversation with Neal. Later sixteen fellows got together and shared about their own lives, and they came to me with a burning question. "All that stuff about Neal is fine for guys who are virgins—clean, spotless guys," they said, "but none of us are in that position. All of us have already disobeyed God. We've had sex with girls. We've failed—does that mean we're through, disqualified from being Christians? Are we ready for the junk pile?"

Of course I told them no. "That's what 1 John 1:9 is all about," I said. "It says if we confess our sins, God will cleanse us from all unrighteousness."

Peter, Jesus' disciple, had the same confusion those guys had. He couldn't get it through his head that God was so forgiving—that every time you blew it, God was glad to forgive you. He asked Jesus, "How many times do you have to forgive a man, seven times?" Jesus said no, seventy times seven, or as many times as he comes to you. Now if God expected Peter to forgive so readily, doesn't it follow that God would at least be that forgiving?

Some people have gotten very good at asking for forgiveness. You wonder how sincere they are, because they haven't changed the situations that made them sin in the first place. Fellows, for instance, complain about trouble with their thought life. Sometimes I have to tell them, "Don't come and talk to me about your thought life. You go home and get rid of your issues of *Playboy* and

Penthouse—the ones you have underneath your dresser drawer or up in the attic. Until you've done that, it's pretty hard to believe you want to clean up your thought life."

We talked about the purpose of prayer in chapter 7. Don't overlook prayer as a great weapon in fighting temptation. If you're going to be with a bunch of kids who you know like to gossip, for instance, pray that you'll be able to have a good time with them and not gossip. Ask God to help you steer the conversation toward better things.

The Bible helps tremendously. If you know the Bible, if you read it, and think about it, there's good material going into you. The old computer slogan, "Garbage in, garbage out," really applies here. If there's garbage going into your mind, garbage is going to come out, too. It helps to read a verse before you go to bed. That gives your mind something to work on while you're asleep.

Temptation demands a positive antidote. You can't waltz into a compromising situation, and then think, "I hope I don't do anything wrong." You need a positive antidote long before then. Get a hobby; get involved; fill up your mind with good things.

And when it comes to resisting temptation, it's amazing how little credit common sense gets. There are practical things you can do in specific situations. If you're tempted to go too far with a girl or guy, for instance, there are specific things you need to watch out for. You start getting into trouble when you plan on spending five hours together, but don't plan what you're going to do. Common sense will tell you what you'll end up doing. If you don't plan your date, and then go too far, don't yell, "The devil made me do it." You asked for trouble.

God wants you to use your head. He wants you to use prayer, to turn to him and his Word when the going gets rough. He wants you to fill your mind and your life with positive, good things. He doesn't want you crushed by the pressures outside your body, but maintained by the Spirit of Christ living inside you. Everyone is tempted, but as 1 Corinthians 10:13 says, no temptation is too great for you to resist. This is God's goal in these pressure situations: by resisting temptation, you'll let him transform you in each area of your life. He wants you to grow as a Christian.

TAKEOFF

When do you feel the greatest struggles with temptation? Make a list of times and situations. During the next week add to that list.

Apply the suggested steps in this chapter to those temptations that create the greatest pressure in your life. 1) Pray for forgiveness where you have failed. 2) Pray specifically about that temptation and ask God for strength to face it the next time. 3) Check the Bible for advice or examples of people who faced a similar temptation. Use a topical Bible. 4) Develop a common sense strategy for handling the temptation next time it hits you. Decide now exactly how you're going to respond.

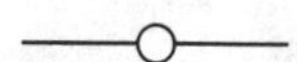

Romans 12:1–2 and Ephesians 6:10–18 offer some general suggestions about handling the world's pressures. You might conduct a character study of the Old Testament prophet, Daniel, if you want to get an encouraging picture of someone who faced terrific pressure to conform.

Coaches, parents, teachers, friends—it seems everybody wants to tell us what to do.
Gregg Lewis

10

Why Can't I Run My Own Life?

Here's a typical scene. You've barely started talking on the telephone when your mother starts getting on you for talking so long. She makes you hang up. You get into an argument. Somewhere in the middle of that argument you realize your sister was on the phone just before you were, and your mother probably heard that and thought it was you. She thinks you've been on the phone all that time. It's too late for that fact to calm things down, though; she's furious at you for talking back, and you go storming out of the room with her yelling at you. Later on you have all kinds of mixed feelings. You feel guilty for mouthing off to your mother, but on the other hand, you know she was wrong. So why should you obey her?

There are similar scenes played out every day in thousands of homes. They bring up a conflict with authority. The parents are supposed to rule the home, but often you'd rather they didn't. The same thing goes on at school between students and teachers. Conflicts between the government and individual citizens come up every time someone gets caught speeding or taking drugs. When you're working and the boss tells you to do something you hate doing, you feel a surge of rebellion. Or how about when there's something you want to do, yet you know God would not want you to? That's another conflict.

There are innumerable sources of authority in your life, constantly telling you what to do. You certainly don't have to feel guilty over rebellious feelings, because they're normal. But when it comes to authority, Christians find most of the time that their duty is to obey. That's one of the most unpopular parts of Christianity. Just about everybody thinks Jesus was a neat person, worth imitating. But when they reach the part of the Bible that says, "Submit yourself to the earthly authorities," they balk.

Freedom is a very popular theme. Everybody wants to be free, and a common popular assumption is that the way to be free is to do only what you feel like. "Don't let anyone box you in with his ideas of what you should do. Do *your* thing." The fewer inhibitions you have and the fewer people you have to obey, the freer you are.

I Could Run My Own Life

I think we have to reject the common idea of freedom. Christians see freedom not as freedom from authority—in which case a wild dog would be freer than any of us—but freedom to do what will ultimately satisfy us in life. That freedom very often comes as a result of being under authority—especially under one particular authority.

We Christians give ultimate authority to one man only—Jesus Christ. That's really what Christianity is. We pray something like this: "Listen, God, I could run my own life, or let it be run according to what my teachers want or what my friends think is good. But I know that won't work. I want you to be the authority. I want you to be Lord in my life." That is the basic step in coming to know Jesus as a person. Obedience is definitely part of being a Christian.

There's more to it than submission to Christ's authority, though. There are other authorities in our lives—our parents, our teachers, the government, our bosses. Just toss them out and let God tell us what to do? That would be fine if we really had a corner on God, and if he really always guided us by whispering commands in our ears. But he doesn't restrict himself to that; he uses human authority to guide us and, incidentally, to impose some order on this world.

Part of the reason many of us resent verses in the Bible that tell us to obey is that we think of authority strictly in terms of commands. Actually, that's just a small part of what the principle of authority is all about. You could think of a car's drive train as an example of authority. The clutch engages, one clutch plate responds to the authority of the other, and the result is that the car can go somewhere. It's really a way of working together; it's a sense of order.

Or think of ordering food in a restaurant. You could be as powerful as the President of the United States, yet you would still need to submit to the authority of the waitress. She tells you where to sit, hands you the menu, and asks what you'd like. If you got up out of your seat and tried to get your own meal, nothing would work correctly.

Honor Your Uncle

I happen to believe that the family is a crucial area of society. If one family falls apart, the split is painful for the individuals, but probably not for anyone else. But if half the families in a school neighborhood or in a country are falling apart, it's going to affect that school, that country. So when we're talking about the principle of authority, making things work together, one of the most crucial areas is right at home. "Honor your father and your mother," the Bible says.

Why should it work that way? Why not honor uncles or aunts? Why not have parents obey children? Well, I don't know precisely why. There may be a certain amount of arbitrariness to it; somebody had to be boss, and it came down to parents.

But in at least one sense it is not arbitrary. We saw in chapter 2 how, in the Bible, God is often referred to as "Father." There's deep wisdom in that. You can't see God, and it is hard to get a grip on what he is like. However, all of us know what fathers are like. Even if you have a poor father or even if your father is dead, you have some sense of the way an ideal father should be, and how you should relate to him.

Fathers are living, breathing facts, and they are facts that God uses to teach us about himself. Specifically, as we learn to submit ourselves in love to our father's authority, not because we have to but because we want to, then we learn how to submit ourselves to God's authority. When you obey your parents, you are learning about obeying (and loving) God. If you consistently refuse to honor your parents, it will be difficult to honor God.

Of course, there is a problem—your parents aren't God. God won't ask you to do what isn't wise, but your parents might. So how do you deal with that?

When you're in the army, they tell you something I believe is helpful. They say, "Don't salute the man, salute the uniform." Plenty of officers will rank above you who aren't worthy of the position they hold. They really don't deserve the respect symbolically represented in a salute. But the system has to be maintained. If every buck private could make up his own mind whom to salute and whom not to salute, the system would fall apart.

Today we're in a culture that has a lot of failure. The tendency is to add up all the failures and make the rules on the basis of them. There are so many bad marriages that we want to throw away marriage as an institution. There are so many bad homes that we'll make new rules under which children run their own lives. There are so many bad schools that we decide children won't have to obey; they can make all the rules themselves.

There's no question that authority gets abused. Some parents, for instance, are overstrict and rigid. But if those mistakes are allowed to define what parents are all about, and therefore parents stop trying to raise kids and let them raise themselves instead, I can promise you general chaos.

True, there are parents who don't deserve your respect. So what do you do? Run away from home? Resent and hate them? Revolt? Those are options, but they're options that place your individual happiness above everything else. Jesus offered a larger rule that takes in all those abuses and exceptions to the system. "Love your enemies," he said. If your father is a tyrant, how do you handle him? Try treating him with respect and love, by expecting proper guidance from him, by acting as though he were the kind of parent you wish he were. Salute the uniform, not the man; respect him as an individual. The surprising thing is that very often that kind of respect and love will bring out just the kind of behavior he should have had in the first place.

One Man Screamed

Our society does fall short of the ideal, and it's easy to accept and grow complacent about that, forgetting the ideal even exists. I remember taking a flight in a twin-engine airplane. In midair one engine quit. Even though the pilot warned us about it and assured us things would be all right, people panicked. One man stood up and cried and screamed. The stewardess was running and comforting people, trying to keep order. Every one of us felt fear in the pit of the stomach. But the plane just kept droning along, and after a while we realized that the pilot was right. We would make it safely. By the time we got to the end of the trip, we'd practically forgotten our fear. It seemed quite normal to be flying with only one engine.

Suddenly it dawned on me that we were getting used to something we had no business getting used to. The plane was badly damaged, but we'd practically forgotten that. It's the same in our society. Families are falling apart, but we change the rules and manage to limp along. Pretty soon we're all acting as though it's normal for half the families to fall apart. It isn't. One job Christians must do in our society is always point the direction back to the ideal that God intended for us. We do that partly by "saluting the uniform"—by recognizing that though, say, your parents aren't the best, respect and authority in a family are very, very important. It's the same thing in interacting with government, with churches, with teachers, with bosses, with anyone who is in authority over you (even waitresses). You respect the individual because you respect the system.

Kings and Soldiers

Of course, there are times to disobey. When my son was little we read the New Testament account of Herod killing the infants. My son asked, "Daddy, didn't the soldiers have babies of their own?"

"Yes," I said.

"Well, was the king bigger than the soldiers?"

"No. They were probably about the same size."

"Well, were there more kings than there were soldiers?"

"No, it was the other way around."

"Daddy," he said, "didn't they know that killing the babies was wrong?"

"Yes," I said, "they probably knew it. But when kings tell soldiers to do something, they do it."

He said, "Daddy, I don't care. If it was wrong, they shouldn't have done it."

This was the central issue behind the Nuremberg trials, in which Nazis were tried for murder. Many of them pleaded innocent on the basis that they were commanded, on penalty of death, to kill helpless Jews. But for a Christian the issue is: Whose authority is supreme? Ultimately, we serve Christ. We disobey whatever tells us to contradict his authority.

That rarely happens. I don't think there are very many times when our government or our parents or our schools tell us to do something contrary to what God wants us to do. But I do know that it happens. For ten years now I've gotten letters from a girl whose father used to insist that she have sex with him three times a week. I told her not to do it. Eventually the situation became so severe that we had to put an ultimatum to him: Either quit or we'd have him committed to an institution. He quit it, and she grew up, left home and now is happily married and has a family.

That's a rare situation, but it does happen. There are conflicts between the authority on earth and God's authority. "We must obey God rather than men."

Beyond that, keep in mind that authority is human. It's not a bunch of inflexible commands. You see that in the Bible. The Bible is not a book of ten thousand sins, but a book full of the experiences of people. Some of those lean in a God-ward way and some lean away from God. We read the long-range results of those leanings. We learn principles, not rules. If God's authority were reducible to a long list of do's and don'ts, then that's what God would have given us. If the laws of our land were reducible to a long list of commands, we wouldn't need judges and juries and presidents and congressmen and governors. We'd just have a couple of volumes called "The Rules." We don't have that. There are always gaps to laws, and that's why the legal libraries of our country are a lot bigger than "The Rules." They try to fill the gaps. But there's still always a need for individuals with wisdom to fill the gaps, and find the exceptions to the rules, and to apply the rules in a sensible way.

And the fact that authority is human means that it makes mistakes. The attitude it takes toward those mistakes makes a huge difference. If leaders try to ignore or get defensive about their mistakes, they automatically draw hostility the way honey draws flies. Attitudes of defensiveness erode rather than strengthen authority. Any authority figure who can face his mistakes openly has gained, not lost.

If you want to help the authorities in your life be more worthy of respect, figure out ways to get them off the defensive. Treat them with respect and honor. Let them know you don't respect them less because they make mistakes. Let them know, by being open about your failures, that they can be open about theirs. Try it with your parents, your teachers, your boss. Over a period of time it will make a difference.

The Principle of Order

Authority is the principle by which order is maintained, the principle which lets people work together. We live in a mixed universe, wherein sin has put people in rebellion against authority, and authority itself is sometimes badly corrupted. But we must not, as Christians, make the mistake of giving up on authority, or of giving up on the ways of working together that God has given us.

Families are important; therefore, obey your parents. Learning from older, wiser people is important; therefore, respect your teachers. We need government; therefore, respect the law and the people who carry it out. The reward that will come if this is done in love is a deeper respect for the God who made all these things, and a deeper harmony in your world.

TAKEOFF

Take a few minutes and try to think of all the people whose authority you are expected to submit to. Which ones are the most difficult to cheerfully obey? When do you have the biggest trouble obeying? Go back through this chapter with these specific people or situations in mind. Mark the points in the chapter that seem most relevant to your struggle.

Think of an authority figure close to you—a parent, a teacher, and so on. In what ways do you show respect to that person now? What specific additional things could you do to show your respect? Put some of those into practice this week.

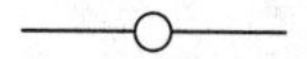

The thirteenth chapter of Romans and Ephesians 5:21–6:9 talk a lot about authority. If you'd like to contrast these Scripture passages with Bible characters who chose the route of civil obedience when they had to choose between God's authority and man's, read the stories of Moses and Daniel.

If we
really care,
we have to
do more than
pray
and talk.
Bob Taylor

11

How Much Do I Need to Give?

In India I began to understand the depth of the problems of poor people. I was walking down a street with a friend when I heard an odd noise behind me. There was a click followed by a swishing sound, then another click and a swish, and more. I turned around to see what it was. I saw a young boy, perhaps twelve years old, whose legs were gone. He had two short, hand-made crutches about eighteen inches long with which he pulled himself along the streets. That made the sound—click when he put down the crutches, swish when he dragged his body over the streets.

He asked me for money. What could I do? I was moved by his situation. I reached into my pocket where I'd collected a number of Indian coins, and I emptied a handful into his hands. I didn't think about the fact that I was probably giving him more than a grown man there earned in several days; I just gave him the coins.

Almost immediately there was a reaction. From doorways and alleys people spilled out, more than I could believe. They attacked the boy, hitting him and jumping on him, taking his money away. I tried to help him, shoving them away while he held onto the money for dear life. But they got most of it. He crawled over to the side of the street with perhaps one or two of the coins left. Strangely, though, he didn't seem very unhappy about the whole affair.

That's a world no person who lives in America can really understand. Naturally, I was upset at the greed that could steal so brazenly from the boy. But what did I know about the kind of life that exists day after day with the serious possibility of starving to death?

But though that world of hunger and poverty is one I can't fully understand, I can't afford to ignore it. Not any longer! The world is changing, and the hungry nations aren't just sitting by passively hoping for a handout. They are becoming more and more outspoken in their demands. They are questioning whether we have any rights to our riches.

Americans are beginning to hear the sounds of the masses just as in the medieval days when men defended castles. Knights then would be trapped inside, looking out through slits in the walls, listening to the pounding of their enemies at the door or the digging at the base of the castle where their enemies tried to make the walls collapse. Today, the rich Western peoples are surrounded by a massive nuclear moat, hoping it will hold off the hungry people outside. More and more we hear the pounding at the door.

Baby on the Doorstep

Increased population is responsible for many of the problems, but I don't think that's the whole story. People have been starving, and dying of diseases, all through history. The real change is the shrinking of the globe—the increased communications. We are aware of people we had never heard of before.

I think any Christian person would respond with love and care to a baby left on his doorstep. If the baby were starving, he would feed it. If the baby were on the road in front of his house, he would still feel a compulsion to go out and feed it. Even put the baby clear down on the end of the block, and he would probably walk to the end of the block to feed it. However, if you move that baby to India, he probably won't feel the same responsibility. But the moral problem is no different. A baby starving in India is no different from a baby starving on our doorstep. And in a sense, with the growth of communication systems like radio and television, the world has become our doorstep. We know about those starving babies; we even see them on TV. And how can we ignore them, let alone ignore the poor and starving of our own country?

That is why I've personally agonized over this question of wealth as much as any other single issue. We have got to evaluate our lifestyle and begin asking ourselves on a personal basis, "Is there a line of richness beyond which I cannot go? Am I really dealing with my responsibility to give time and money to others? Do I really love, or do I only love those people when it's painless?" We are the richest people in the history of the world. It only makes sense that our greatest temptations should come in the area of wealth.

The One-Camel Family

The Bible doesn't raise this question in quite the way it's raised today. Its first concern isn't whether a Christian ought to own one camel or two. It talks first of all about the philosophy of materialism—the "ism" that says the world is simply material, and that's all there is to it. The answer to any problem, according to this philosophy, lies in material, and that's why a genuine materialist puts his faith in material goods.

I believe Jesus is attacking materialism in Matthew 6 when he says, "Don't store up treasures here on earth where they can erode away or may be stolen. Store them in heaven where they . . . are safe from thieves." He talked about the transitory nature of things—that someday this very planet will be used up, finished—but said there are living, eternal qualities, spiritual things, that will go on forever. In 1 Corinthians 13 Paul talks about the things that won't last, and he even includes things like knowledge and the ability to communicate. The only things that will last, he concludes, are faith, hope, and love—spiritual qualities with eternal significance. The person who thinks "things" are the key to life is on the wrong track.

But there is also a second concern you find in the Bible. I heard Richard Halverson, who was then pastor of Fourth Presbyterian Church in Washington, D.C., speak about this. He said he had taken out a concordance and done an exhaustive study of what the Bible has to say about wealth and about the poor. One thing stood out to him. He said he found that unrighteousness and neglect of the poor are virtually synonymous in the Bible. When the Bible talks about the kind of life that God loves to see, it virtually always includes something about caring for oppressed and poor people. When Israel was in trouble in the Old Testament, she would often accelerate her worship, her Bible reading, and prayer. But that wasn't what God was looking to see. He saw that the neglect of the poor continued, and he would judge and condemn her.

I concur fully with Halverson's feelings. If we're to look honestly at what the Bible says, we have to conclude that the way we deal with the poor is integrally tied with a healthy response to God.

Of course, you meet a lot of people who are very concerned about the poor, but often it seems to be all talk. Their sacrifices are minimal. They don't give up money or time when it really hurts. Some people who talk well can't even find time for the needs of the people next door. Or they may find money to give to the poor, but they don't have any time to give. Most of the poor I know would prefer that you befriend them and care for them as people rather than that you drop off some money. There is a world of difference between the person who is philosophically committed to dealing with the problems of poverty and the person who has really made himself vulnerable by acting on his beliefs. This is what God wants.

But with real commitment, problems come. The situation is very much more complex than it seems at first. Like my experience in India—I thought I was doing something kind in giving money to the beggar boy. However, human greed destroyed most of the good I'd intended for him. The same is true of other things on a much larger scale. With the increase in population, there is the really serious question whether *any* amount of giveaways would forestall starvation. Perhaps it even eventually makes things worse, by allowing people to survive now and starve in greater numbers later.

And then there are the factors of bureaucracy and greed. Suppose I gave my dollar to a volunteer agency. Suppose I decided not to eat hamburgers at Burger King because beef is a very inefficient producer of protein. How is that really going to affect the baby in Bangladesh? Will my dollar be eaten up by politicians or by greedy merchants? Even if it gets there, will it be a drop in the bucket, a meaningless crumb in the face of a problem that is bigger than I am, perhaps bigger than the resources of the entire world?

Sell All and Give to the Poor

What can I do that will make a difference? Should I give up all my money and live in total, abject poverty? There was a point in my life where I tried that. My wife Janie and I had almost nothing—we gave it all away. For years I lived in basements and attics. I gave that lifestyle up because I couldn't see how it was doing anyone any good. I'd given up so much I'd disqualified myself from helping anyone. I didn't even have the gas to get out of my driveway to go help someone. I had given everything away.

At another point, later on, I had the desire to move into a ghetto in Chicago to see if I could pick up cans and bottles from my yard as quickly as people could throw them there. But as I thought about that, I realized I'd be putting pressure on my wife and kids rather than on myself. And would it really solve anything? And if I were to sell all and give to the poor, then how poor would I want to become? Do I want to identify with the poor of a Chicago ghetto? By certain African or Indian standards, American poverty is gaudily rich. Do I go all the way and starve to death, identifying with the poor of Bangladesh? If so, what good have I done? These are the agonizing questions I've asked myself time and again.

I don't think I've come up with any final answer, and so far as I can see no one else has either. I am fairly sure that there is no absolute answer for everyone; that what is right for one person may not be right for someone else. And I am also fairly sure that giving everything away and joining the counter-culture is not the answer to the problems of poverty. I don't help anyone by buying a pair of K-Mart blue jeans and living from hand to mouth, maybe even begging from people on the street and then criticizing them for their lifestyle. I don't help anyone by living off the land in a commune or living off a compassionate father who sends me money. I have concluded that there are real advantages to the kind of life that punches a clock and earns a living producing something worthwhile.

So what do I do, beyond earning a living and maybe sending off a check to Compassion or World Vision? I once felt you could change the world just by changing individuals. I'd go beyond that now. I'm more and more convinced that the world is changed when you change individuals who commit themselves to changing institutions, which then change the world. Government in particular is going to be, in our age, the primary agency through which the starving are fed or not fed.

I hope that when I hear politicians talking about "rugged individualism" and "America first," I will react immediately by saying, "This is not a Christian way of looking at life." God says we should love our brothers, and I am committed to doing that politically as well as personally.

They Die One at a Time

At the same time, I know government will never solve a problem people aren't willing to combat themselves, individually. I know that for the man without work reducing the overall percentage of unemployment hardly helps. You are either employed or you are unemployed—helping unemployed people happens one person at a time. No one ever increased his employment 3 percent just because the government statistics said it happened. The same with starving people—you either have enough food or you don't. People die one at a time. Even if one person can't help everybody, all help must begin with a single individual and a single act. If I can't offer money, I can offer dignity. If I can't offer food, I can offer time.

And of course, one of the positive things about the free-enterprise system is that I can go out, starting with a little money, and generate a large amount of money if I'm successful. It may be that's the role some of us should play. After all, someone had to start Ford Motor Company—why not have it be someone who's committed to using the profits to feed hungry people rather than to buy yachts? There is a place for individual initiative, whether it's developing a business whose profits might help poor people, or whether it's moving into the ghetto to work on a project of immediate significance in helping people.

Personally, I know God hasn't called me to do either of those things. The chief thrust of my life is to work on the task of leading people to Jesus Christ. And most of us simply aren't going to be called into the ghetto, or into politics, or into big finance. Most of us are going to be accountants and carpenters and secretaries and teachers—jobs where we have limited amounts of money and limited amounts of influence.

But there are things that we can do to fulfill our social responsibility. For one thing, we can be sensitive to the problem politically. We can also give what we're able to give. And that raises the issue of how we live. We have, in my family, tried to stress two principles: "make do" and "simplify." When we want to replace something, we really ask hard, "Can we 'make do' with what we have? Can it last another year? Or can we find some ways to fix up the old thing so that it works well?"

And then we look for ways to simplify. This isn't just in the interests of saving money. It's in the interests of our own sanity. I've found that many so-called labor-saving devices are actually terribly consuming. You have to keep fixing them when they break down. You constantly put them away and take them out again. Gadgets complicate your life; they don't simplify it.

Poor Materialists

The question to me is, What dollars can I free productively to do what God wants? There are those who think that money itself is the big evil—that you have to get rid of it so it won't soil you or seduce you into sin. I don't think they know what they are talking about. I've been poor most of my life, grew up poor and lived around relatively poor people. I know I've met just as many materialists among the poor as among the rich. It's tempting to care about nothing but money when you're poor. It's easy to think that if you just had enough money, all your problems would be solved. But that is a total illusion.

Actually I've met more people among the sons and daughters of rich people who knew how much it was an illusion. They have drunk from the wells of money and have found the water acrid. It doesn't satisfy. Many, out of laziness and habit, may continue to live the same life. But many others become aware of the spiritual dimensions of life and of their responsibility to use money wisely. That may take a different form from what you'd expect. They may not give it all away and go live in a shack. Instead, they may be plowing it back into the business. But is it just greed making them do that? Not always.

I know a man who is the head of a very large company, one of the finest men I have ever met. Every day when he gets up, his first thought is that he must do his best to keep his company healthy. Why? Because he is intensely aware that many thousands of people depend on that for their jobs, and he feels he can't let them down. It's not so that he'll make more money, either: he has more money than he will ever need, and he's given huge sums of it away. But he feels that God has given him a lot to be responsible for, and his duty is to take that responsibility with great seriousness. Other people's lives depend on him.

All of us have been given some area of responsibility—people, money, things—that we have charge of. We can use them in the way a Christian ought to, or we can forget about relating them to God and go our own way, driven by impulses or greed. Those to whom God has given a lot have a special responsibility—nearly an awesome responsibility. I believe that this is what Jesus referred to when he said, "It is easier for a camel to go through the eye of a needle than for a rich man to enter the Kingdom of God." I think he was talking about a real camel and a real needle, the kind you sew with.

What Jesus is saying is this: It may well be that your lifestyle can demonstrate where your heart really is. If seven-tenths of the world is starving, and you are rich, how you deal with that situation may indicate how you're dealing with Christ himself. Do you really love him more than your money? You say you do—but do you put your money on the line? James 2:14–26 develops this same idea when it says faith without works is dead. James doesn't mean that unless you act right God won't love you. He means that the overall pattern of your life may tell a lot about what your real relationship with the Lord is.

Sitting on top of all our material things, secure financially, it's easy to talk about God. It may be that the discrepancy between the rich and the poor is a test, a test to see if we really understand what spiritual life is, and are willing to follow it.

In fact, I've often wondered why God allows these four

things on this earth: natural calamities like earthquakes or floods, sickness, the problem of race, and the problem of poverty. What's so important about these, that he couldn't have designed the world a little differently?

One reason may be that these are the final exams for life. Take race as an obvious example. God could have made us all purple. Instead, he made us with various shades of color. Why? It's a test to see whether we really understand that love is not stopped by personal differences. Real Christian love isn't concerned with the color of someone's skin. If you say you love God but consistently hate your brother of another color, you're wrong in what you say about loving God. Your attitude toward others has shown it. The same is true if you say you love God, yet that love never seems to stir up any real compassion toward the poor, never really hurts your pocketbook. Your actions speak louder than your words.

The Final Word

We live in the richest country in the history of the world. Despite all economic problems we undergo, that remains true. And the Bible says, "From the person to whom much has been given, much will be required." We have been given a great deal—and with it goes a great responsibility. I wish there were hard-and-fast answers to the problems of social responsibility, rules like, "Join the poverty ranks," or "Give a straight 10 percent tithe, no more, no less." But those answers aren't enough. I believe this is a problem every individual must struggle with, discussing it openly with his Christian friends and with God, studying the Bible and letting it determine the way he acts.

How much do I need to give? The answers we find are going to be different ones—I know that in advance. The crucial questions to me are, "Are we wrestling with the problems at all? And are we acting?" For the way we handle our possessions has always been one of God's concerns. His Gospel contains social as well as spiritual implications. And for those of us who are rich in a world of poverty, his concern must be very great.

If you're in high school or college, you may doubt this applies to you. But it does. You have responsibility for a lot—not so much as your parents perhaps, but far more than a kid in India. What will you do with it? You are on the training grounds of life.

TAKEOFF

One of the most valuable responses to this chapter might be to do a little thinking about values. So imagine that you are going to be shipwrecked on a remote island by yourself for the rest of your life. If you could take ten things with you, what would they be? If you could take five? Three? How many of the things on your list of ten reflect materialistic values? Why do you think it's so easy to be materialistic?

When was the last time you gave anything to, or did something for, someone who was in need? What are some practical goals you could set in this area?

Witnessing isn't just what you say or do, it's what you are.

Kay Freeman

12

How Do I Tell Others About My Faith?

I became a Christian while I was in high school. It was like fireworks going off in my life. Overnight I felt different. I acted differently.

I guess I followed a typical pattern. I learned from other Christians that I was supposed to witness, to tell people about Jesus. And I went at it wholeheartedly. I told everybody I talked to that he needed to be saved. If I went somewhere and failed to tell somebody about his eternal destiny, I'd feel guilty.

You don't have to be a genius to figure out what happened. People were turned off. Pretty soon they didn't want to talk with me. They weren't inviting me to parties, and they weren't enthusiastic about spending time with me. Even my family was alienated.

I thought this was proof of how pure I was: "What have the children of light to do with the children of darkness?" I told myself they were rejecting God, not me. And I kept on busily talking to everybody I could buttonhole.

Years later I woke up. I realized I had erected barriers between myself and former friends. I couldn't talk about anything but religion. I'd become a self-centered fanatic. I thought people were rejecting God, while actually they weren't closed at all to Christ. They just didn't want to become weird like me.

That's when I went back and began rebuilding the bridges I'd destroyed. I'd had no time to simply be *friends* with those people. I'd been too busy witnessing to be interested in things they were interested in. I'd had no time to laugh, cry, celebrate with them. Consequently, they wouldn't listen to me. It's only fair, really. I wasn't listening to them, why should they listen to me?

As I rebuilt those bridges, I was also studying the Bible. I noticed a very interesting thing there about the word "witness." For me, to "witness" was to get some tracts and go out and talk to people. It was something I did. But the Bible didn't use "witness" that way very much. "Witness" was a noun much more often that it was a verb. A "witness" was a person who had Jesus Christ in his life.

Gradually it dawned on me. I didn't have to go out on the streets and preach to be a witness. I *was* a witness. I didn't have any choice in the matter. The day I accepted Jesus Christ into my life, I became a witness. People could look at me and say, "So that's what God does to people."

That changed everything. You see, I had the idea that you heard a sermon and got charged up, and then you went out and gave this spiel. If you were a good speaker, could think clearly, and knew the right techniques, then you were a "good witness."

But witnessing isn't just what you do, it's also what you are. So what is a "good" witness? A good witness must be roughly the same as a good person, measured by Christ's standards. A good witness is somebody you want to be with. A good witness is somebody whose style of life shows that Christ is having an effect on his life. He shows it not only in what he says, but in what he does.

My New Car

I remember the first time I ever owned a brand-new car. I was proud. I couldn't wait for my wife to send me to the store for a quart of milk so I could show it off. I'd drive slowly past friends' houses, wave to people—I wanted everyone to see I had a new car.

A good witness has that kind of natural enthusiasm. You don't worry so much about how and when to say things as much as *being*. You concentrate on Jesus Christ. Then when you talk, you're sharing the joy and love you've found—not some packaged message that belongs to someone else.

There's a beautiful example of that kind of witness in Acts 3 and 4. Peter and John were on their way to the temple, and they healed a lame beggar on the way. It caused quite a stir, which ended when Peter and John were arrested and forbidden by the authorities to spread their message. Peter and John said, "You decide whether God wants us to obey you instead of him! We cannot stop telling about the wonderful things we saw Jesus do and heard him say."

We can be like them. People might laugh at us for talking about God; they might give us a hard time. But we ignore those reasons. We obey God—and we cannot stop telling about the wonderful things Jesus does and says.

But that means talking about what Jesus means to *you*. If your heart is empty, if your Christian life really doesn't mean much to you, if you don't have any joy or fulfillment in life, don't go trying to give it to other people. But if God *is* doing something in your life, then you'll want to tell about it.

There will be other urges, too—fear and shyness. They will make you want to be quiet. But hopefully, they will be balanced by the basic urge to share something good with people you care about. That is the urge you should pay attention to.

Holy Hammerlock?

Suppose you want to share what God is doing. How do you go about it? Get a hammerlock on every person who comes near you and talk his ear off?

No. Rely on God to work. I used to force my way into situations. Now I know that the Holy Spirit will open doors for me if I ask. Try starting your day by praying, "Please open up some opportunities for me to share my trust in you." You can pray for specific people this way, too: "Please let some of the time we spend talking turn to serious things." I've found that when I do that, God will consistently open things up in a beautiful way. People will say, "Boy, I just don't know how it was you who happened my way." But I know. It was the Holy Spirit going ahead of me.

Just as important as prayer is knowing what your goals are.

"I know what I want," you say. "I want my friends to become Christians." But think that out. All of us tend to want everybody else just like us. We have a cookie-cutter approach. We want everyone molded to the shape we think a Christian ought to have. If you look closely at the mold you're using, it usually looks a lot like your own face.

That approach doesn't even make copies. All it communicates is, "I'm good and you're bad. I'm going to heaven and you're going to hell. I'm an insider; you're an outsider." That doesn't excite people about Jesus. Nobody wants to be treated like a welfare case.

You have to build bridges to other people in order to communicate. The good news about Jesus is a heavy message: It takes a strong bridge. The strongest bridge is what I call an "I care" bridge. "I care about you as a person," it says. "I'm not telling you this just to get another notch in my belt."

"You're Going to Hell"

How do you build that kind of bridge? One thing's for sure, you can't pretend you're interested in someone just so you can get your message across. They'll spot you as a phony sooner or later. No, if you don't care about other people as persons—not targets—you'd better start praying God will make you care about them. He's the only one who can.

After that, building bridges is just like building any friendship. You listen to others. You show an interest in what they care about. You show flexibility by doing what they want some of the time.

I know of a girl who went to her Campus Life club director and said she'd tried everything to win her school to Christ, and they were just laughing at her. So he asked her what she'd done.

"Well," she said, "I go early every day and put tracts in lockers telling the kids they're going to hell. Then at noon hour, I take my Bible and stand in back of the school. I preach to them and tell them they're lost."

The club director made her promise to stop preaching and putting tracts in their lockers. He said, "Just try an experiment. Do you know of any one person you'd particularly like to reach?"

She thought about it. There was one girl she was particularly concerned about.

"Well, what does she like to do?" he asked.

"She likes to swim, I guess. She goes to the YMCA a lot."

So he told her to start swimming with her.

"But I don't like to swim," she said.

"Well," he said, "maybe she doesn't like to be a Christian."

So she began to go to the Y with this other girl. She went for five or six weeks, and nothing happened. Finally one day the girl turned to her and said, "Why are you doing this?"

Then she told her she liked her and thought she was a fine person, and she shared her faith. For the first time the girl was really interested in hearing it. She said to the Christian girl, "I used to think you were weird. Now I can see you're a real person!"

That's the kind of attitude you want to communicate. You don't want to say, "Become exactly like me." It's more, "We're both beggars going hungry, and I've found out where they give away food. I want to share it."

The Big Hurt

I was in a church in Chicago a few years ago, and when I was leaving I walked out to my car and found a man leaning against it. He asked me if I had a minute.

He said, "I want to share something with you, Jay. Tell me why this is: I've been in this church thirty years. I've been a deacon; I've gone door-to-door talking to people; I've done just about everything. And all these years I've never really led anyone to Christ."

He went on to tell me that the year before his son had gotten into trouble. He had raped a girl in the neighborhood. It got into the papers. Everybody knew about it. He and his wife were ashamed to go to church, ashamed even to go out of their house. Finally they decided they couldn't hide from the world forever, so they started back to church.

"Do you know what's happened?" he said. "In the last year at least half a dozen men have come to me in private, told me their deepest problems, and asked me for help. I've had more chances to talk to people in one year than I had in thirty. Now why is that?"

"Why do you think it is?" I said.

"Maybe," he said, "it's because people want help from someone they know needed help of his own. Maybe they feel that because you have been hurt you'll understand them when they are hurt." He thought a little more, and said, "You know, Jay, it was an awful thing to have happen, and I'd never want it to happen again. But maybe it had to happen so I could learn this lesson. People put up a front trying to appear perfect, and they're cutting themselves off from the chance they have to help other people."

Ask yourself, "What kind of help are people looking for?" For instance, if you get a D on a test, who do you look for—a kid with an A? Or do you look around for a kid with a D or an F? You probably find the other kid who failed and go commiserate over a Coke with him.

The world is not waiting for the perfect Christian with all the answers to ride in on his white horse and say, "Be like me." People are looking for someone who has problems like theirs but is working them out. A person who honestly says he has faith in Christ but admits he's facing difficulties, who says he doesn't have all the answers, will communicate. He'll communicate as a real human being. Only robots don't have problems. Just testify up to the level of your own faith. Don't try to put on a faith bigger than what you have. Be honest. Don't chicken out and say less than you believe, but don't pretend and say *more* than you honestly can.

As Intimate As Bad Breath

Though our society is a lot more liberated in some ways than it was a few decades ago, some things are considered as bad as ever. As TV tells us, one of the worst things you can imagine is somebody coming up to you and saying, "You have bad breath."

Well, if breath is that intimate, the soul is at least equally intimate. If you're going to talk to someone about his soul, you surely will want to be as tactful as you would be talking to him about his breath. You're not just talking about social disgrace; you're talking about eternal disgrace.

Choosing an appropriate time to speak is part of this. Do you approach someone when he's in a group of people? Not if you're smart. Few people are willing to talk about intimate things when friends are standing around threatening their self-esteem.

The same is true of arguing. People aren't usually open to changing their minds when they might lose face. If you disagree with a teacher, you don't have to start arguing in class. Come around later and say, "I appreciate what you said, but I've thought about it this way." It's just common sense that you'll get farther by being polite. Avoid putting the other person in an awkward spot.

And make sure what you claim to be faith isn't fear in disguise. Are you afraid of what the other person has to say? Afraid of the weakness of your own position? It always shows through as defensive, and it undermines what you say. Some people have the attitude, "When you're unsure, yell louder." But that doesn't communicate. The only person who can afford to be quiet and calm is the person who is confident in his beliefs.

Guerrilla Tactics

A good witness is never worried about being in the minority. In fact, he knows he's in trouble the minute he gets a majority consensus.

The New Testament idea is that one individual is like yeast in the dough. A little bit goes a long way toward permeating everything around it.

The Christian is called to be that little bit of yeast. He knows he's in the minority, but it doesn't bother him. He believes he has truth on his side, and he inserts truth in situations and lets it grow and cause things to happen. He speaks out against racism, against hatred, against lust, not just by what he says but by the way he acts. By doing that he becomes a good witness. A person who knows him is an eyewitness to what God does.

These are minority tactics. The New Testament doesn't teach people how to run things, or how to violently overthrow the rotten system. It teaches quiet people how to move into others' lives and plant powerful ideas in their minds. When you go into a school, you don't expect everything to be just the way you want it. That doesn't mean you go around eating martyr pills all the time, giving people reasons to hate you. But it does mean certain things will never be popular on this earth, and we shouldn't expect them to be.

I own a book that lists the ten rules Ho Chi Minh had for his soldiers in Vietnam. They're very simple rules: things like, when you go into a house, take off your shoes; never kill a chicken inside the house; never touch a woman. They stress politeness more than military strength. It doesn't sound like a powerful strategy. But it won over more villages than huge tanks did. The tank seemed powerful, but what was happening behind the scenes was different. The whole philosophy of guerrilla warfare is based on getting inside people's heads, not overpowering them.

By that standard, the Bible is a manual for guerrilla warfare. There are instructions like "Love your enemy; do good to those who despise you and use you. Turn the other cheek; walk the second mile." Those are minority tactics. They catch people off guard. They speak louder than words.

Help, I'm a Failure!

When I became a Christian I got the idea that unless everybody I knew became a Christian, I must be some kind of failure. I ran around like crazy doing everything I could, and then doing some more. And I still felt it wasn't enough.

It didn't occur to me that by my standards Jesus Christ was a failure. Most of the people he contacted never put their faith in him.

Christ himself limited his work. He didn't draw on some superhuman strength so he could preach day and night. He limited himself to relatively short times. There were no all-night meetings. He got into boats to avoid the crowd. You don't see Christ chasing people down, buttonholing them, pushing them down with one knee on their throat to force his message down.

He didn't act like that because he trusted his Father to work on those people and to show him the things that really needed doing. He believed that his Father wanted to give rest, not exhaustion. We should be the same way.

Can Openers

I've mentioned how to ask God to prepare situations for sharing Christ, and how to build bridges of caring to people. I've suggested you ought to share what's happened to you, and be honest in what you say.

But I haven't said a word about the can openers.

Can openers are the little booklets, tracts, or outlines you memorize and use when you witness. They are very helpful. *The Four Spiritual Laws* is one popular booklet. *The Roman Road,* a series of verses in Romans that clearly spells out the message of God's salvation, is another. There are others. I don't particularly recommend any one over another, but I do recommend you find one you're comfortable with, and learn it. You might think it'll restrict you, but my experience is that it frees you. It keeps you from talking about a lot of irrelevant stuff when you share your faith and makes sure you remember the crucial data.

But I will offer one word of caution. To hear some people, can openers *are* evangelism. They're not. The witness to Christ is you. No gimmick can do it for you.

But it can help. That's why I call them can openers. They help open the subject and get you past the awkwardness. They bring the crucial stuff out into the open so you can talk about it.

If you want to know more about the specifics, I'd suggest you read Paul Little's book, *How to Give Away Your Faith*.

Most of all, I'd like to stress the point I started with. A witness is a noun before it is a verb. It is what you are as much as what you do.

If you study the Scriptures, you will see three levels of communication God and his people used to communicate his message. Those three levels summarize what I've been saying in this chapter.

One level is *proclamation*—telling. God spoke to people in the Bible. His followers, in everyday conversation, prophesied, preached, and also shared their beliefs. And God expects us to be willing to verbalize our faith, to talk about what he means to us whenever we can do so in a natural, unoffensive way.

The second level is *relational.* God shared his message in the Old Testament partly by relating to the Israelites as their father. Much of what Jesus preached he also showed in the way he treated other people—like Zaccheus and the prostitute who anointed his feet with oil. Those "I care" bridges I talked about say as much, or more, about our faith as our words. They prove what we say.

The third scriptural level of communicating spiritual truth is the *incarnational* level. God sent Jesus to the earth to *be* the most powerful proof he could offer of his love. Jesus was a witness by being an example of the message. And if we are living in Christ, we should *be* a witness just by the kind of people we are and are becoming. Our character should back up what we say and the way we relate to others.

Of course, different people have different strengths in the three ways of communicating. But all three levels are essential.

All through life, in thousands of ways, people should learn about Jesus Christ by our words, our caring, and our character.

That's how God expects us to witness.

TAKEOFF

If the people around you watched carefully, in what ways would your life witness to them? What would they see that wouldn't be a very good witness?

Reread the section of the chapter on the importance of building bridges as the first step in witnessing. Think of someone you'd like to reach, and plan some bridge-building steps you can take. Ask God to help you make those positive contacts.

Evaluate your own effectiveness as a witness in terms of the three levels of communication—proclamational, relational, and incarnational. Do you use all three? How? Why not? Which areas need work?

In addition to the Scripture references in the chapter, you might find helpful insights into witnessing in these: Jesus talking to the woman at the well—John 4:5–29, Philip and the Ethiopian—Acts 8:26–40, and Andrew bringing his brother Peter to Jesus—John 1:37–42. You can read about the time Peter blew his chance to witness in Matthew 26:34–35 and 69–75. And then there's the Great Commission in Matthew 28:19–20.

There can be no such thing as a Christian alone.

J. Fred Sharp

13

What Good Is Church?

It's happened a number of times in the last few years. A young person in high school or college has approached me about starting a Bible study at our house. "Hey, Jay, do you think we could use your home?"

I'll say, "When did you have in mind?" and he'll say, a lot of the time, "How about Sunday?" As we talk, I find out that what he really has in mind is starting a substitute for church, a kind of youth church. Of course, none of them plans on excluding anyone else, but when you dig under the surface, each one wants a group that is composed of people like him: same age, same interests, same problems, same political views.

When you go beyond that and question what they're doing, you find that they're basically unhappy with the established churches. Often the politics bugs them; the churches they've attended seem to think a particular brand of politics and Christianity go hand in hand, and they don't buy that.

Or it may be the style of worship they don't like. They feel they should be accepted in blue jeans, and the church favors dresses and coats and ties. They want to be spontaneous, and the church has an established order of worship. They want contemporary music, and the church likes old hymns. They don't fit in, they don't feel they're being listened to, and consequently they want to meet with a group of people like them.

Not that most young people want to start their own church. Most kids I've met aren't troubled about church. It's not a gut-level issue with them, for one of two reasons: Either they don't go, or they turn it off. They form a mutual nonaggression pact with their parents. I had this sort of thing when I was young. Mom would say, "You can stay up all hours on Saturday night, but you've got to get up and go to church on Sunday morning." It didn't matter what I got out of church. If I could get my body into a vertical position in church Sunday morning, I met her conditions. The same with a lot of churchgoers. They've bought peace at home. It's a small payment, really—two hours on Sunday to get your parents off your back for the rest of the week.

The Lone Ranger

Of these two groups—those who want to form their own "youth" church, and those who sit in church wondering who's winning between the Steelers and the Patriots—I'd have to say I'm drawn closer to the first. At least they care. At least they look at church and expect something from it.

I will never make it as a Christian alone. In fact, there is no such thing as a Christian completely alone. A built-in part of Christianity is being in fellowship, gathering to worship God with people who believe in him.

Of course, what the Bible calls "the church" isn't a building, or a set of doctrinal beliefs, or something officially announced in the bulletin. The church is the believers in Christ, throughout the world, and specifically, the church is the believers who gather in each area—each town, each neighborhood. They may gather in a house, they may meet in the woods, they may meet in a cathedral

—they're still the church. So the fact that the "youth" church wants to meet in my living room doesn't bother me. What bothers me is that it's an attempt to get away from problems that, sooner or later, must be faced.

You see, I've watched a number of these small groups progress. Interestingly enough, the members don't stay young. They tend to get older year by year. Some of them marry and have kids. Well, then John and Mary can't come, because their baby is crying all the time. Ted and Alicia have a baby, and the same problem comes up. The rest of the group doesn't like not seeing those four, so they discuss getting a sitter. Eventually they get volunteers to take care of the children at different meetings.

When their kids get older, they begin to wonder if having them play with Tinkertoys all the time is the best option. "Maybe we should try to teach them about Jesus?" So they try teaching them in various ways, and they stumble over a technique that holds their attention pretty well: flannelgraphs. Pretty soon you have a whole Sunday school setup.

Then there's the building. At some point it usually gets pretty crowded in the living room you're meeting in. The furniture gets scratched. Sometimes the people who own the house are out of town, and that makes complications. So, you rent a hall somewhere. But there are always conflicts with that, too: other people want to use the building at the same time, and the rent gets expensive, and the facilities aren't quite right. Ninety percent of these groups build a church building within about twenty years. Other changes come. Soon you have a group that's evolved into something that looks a lot like what we call the establishment church, except that it took twenty years to get there.

Homogenized?

I have a couple of cautions about that process. First of all, why put all that time and energy into something that ends up looking like what you set out to escape? If that's the result, why not work on changing the bad things instead of starting over? In twenty years you might end up with some changes that are pretty good. That makes a twenty-year head start on the "youth" church.

The other problem is tied up with the whole question of what the church is, and what it's meant to be. Is the church meant to be perfect, constantly enjoyable, never grating? I don't believe so.

In my view, the church is not a homogeneous group. People don't and shouldn't have all the same age, the same political views, the same income, the same skin color, the same politics, or the same basic approach to life. I know there's a lot of talk these days about churches with homogeneous congregations; and I know such churches have real appeal. But I think when you have a congregation where everyone is pretty much alike, you miss out on one of God's primary purposes for the church.

I see the church's job as being something like making ball bearings. To make ball bearings, you get a whole bunch of fairly rough pieces of metal, and you put them in a centerless grinder. Then you get an abrasive like diamond dust or carborundum, and you add it along with a lot of oil. You spin the whole thing with tremendous speed, and the oil moves things around while the metal grates against metal and abrasive. Those imperfect little pieces of metal are ground into bright, perfect little ball bearings.

The church is the same way. You take the young and the old, the wise and the ignorant, and you give them real life experiences. They can't just sit around in an ivory tower talking about Bible verses in a theoretical way. That wouldn't do any good. But if you deal with the real implications of Christ's life in things like family, sex, jobs, worship, and money, you are going to wear on each other. The love of God is the oil—it makes it possible for the surfaces to wear on each other without burning each other up. Everything spins around, and we're able to rub the rough edges off one another.

I may have a particular political view, but in trying to understand the other guy in a loving way, I find that he has something to say. I develop tolerance and patience, things that God really likes to see, if I'm the impatient type. If I'm the complacent type, the impatient people tend to stir me up. All together we mix and wear on each other so we can become a community. In a way, the imperfections in the church are what make it useful. If we're all the same, we may agree and have a good time, but we never grow.

How Long Is a Foot?

If that's what the church is meant to be, then it makes sense that there ought to be all kinds of people in it—the more kinds the better—so as to balance each other. Unfortunately, our society isn't constructed that way, and so neither are churches, because churches aren't synonymous with the kingdom of God. They tend to reflect society at large. Our society tends to be divided along racial lines; so are churches. Our society tends to separate the upper classes from the lower classes. So do churches.

And, of course, there are national and geographic boundaries, so that we in America lose the balancing, shaping influence of, say, African Christians. Our ball bearings tend to develop bulges on one side, because they have an out-of-balance perspective. If everyone in your church is from a rich background, everyone tends to have a rich man's point of view, a view not necessarily in line with the truth. The same is true of a group of believers in a poor neighborhood.

Is everything about the shaping process relative? Does it just depend on the background of the people in the church? It often does, sadly. But it doesn't have to. Two factors can change that. The first is recognizing the outside factors that have determined how you think. Your feelings and ideas do tend to be a creation of your background. If you like having a good car, it's a bet your parents do, too. If classical music isn't your thing, it probably isn't your parents', either. Once you realize that a lot of outside factors influenced your ideas, you become more open to change.

More important, I think, is the fact that we have a standard to bring our ideas up against. That standard is the Word of God—the Bible. Everyone, no matter how much he's broadened his base of experience, still has ideas that are a result of his own relative experience.

But you go to church not to be led by a man, but to be led by Christ. At the Bureau of Standards they have measurements that are the ultimate standards. How do you know exactly how long a foot is? Every yardstick is off a little, because there's human and machine error in it. But if you want to know how long a foot is, they have a ruler at the Bureau of Standards that is exactly a foot. Nobody, no matter how powerful he or she is, can argue with that ultimate standard. No one can change it.

When we come before the Word of God, it's like that. All of us are equal before God—the smart and the slow, the wise and the foolish, the rich and the poor. At church, the idea is to bring our relativistic ideas and measure them against the Word of God. The Holy Spirit works in our lives to help us understand that measure. We adjust our ideas and our lives accordingly, and are brought to a basis of agreement. It doesn't mean we won't differ. God doesn't intend to make us exactly identical. But we do have a standard to bring our own ideas before—something that corrects us, and tells us when we're really out of whack.

Revolution

Not everyone in your church is likely to see things in those idealistic terms. It's sad, but few older people listen to young people with the idea of growing through what's being said. They want them to conform, to "straighten up."

I said before that the church isn't synonymous with the kingdom of God. It's partly a human institution, fallible just as everything else is in our world. It tends to be a microcosm of society in general. That's why it doesn't surprise me a great deal to know that young people have a hard time adjusting and fitting into the church. They have a hard time adjusting and fitting into society in general.

But assuming that you believe what the Bible says, that the church is the place where we're supposed to grow as believers in Christ, then it seems to me there are three possible ways to approach it.

The first option is the revolutionary one. You tear down or bypass the system and build another. The only trouble is, you find most revolutionaries end up looking just like what they were revolting against. That's what happens in the "youth" church we were discussing earlier—you go off and start over, but end up exactly where you were before.

Another option is to get inside the structure of the system and try to change it from within. You play the game, in other words, and gain enough power and influence to have things your own way. A warning though: Before long you may adopt the same characteristics you wanted to change. You become eaten up by the system. "We have met the enemy and he is us," in the immortal words of Pogo.

But there is a third option, what I call modeling. I believe it's what Jesus did. Jesus really wasn't much of a revolutionary, despite what some say. He did not take on the system to radically change it, at least not in the usual "revolutionary" way. On the other hand, he wasn't much of a joiner. He didn't go study and work his way up to being chief priest, then gradually bring in reforms. No, what Jesus did was act as a living example of another way. He represented the kingdom of God, and people who observed him were struck with another alternative in life.

In a smaller way, this is what you should do when you go to church. If you believe you have a greater capacity for tolerance, love, and understanding than your bigoted, conservative elders, show it by being more tolerant. Show it by sitting and listening for long periods of time, by waiting, by turning the other cheek, by being a model of what a Christian is. When you turn the other cheek, you're giving the intolerant man the chance to see a new way of acting. You've unsettled him. Maybe he never lets you know that. Maybe it takes a long time before he realizes, "You know, that young man acts different. . . ." Does it matter? This is the way to make a difference in a loving way, and to bring about changes that come from the heart—changes that are really changes, not just changes on the surface.

Don't Sit in a Corner

I'm not suggesting you go sit in a corner and think nice thoughts, hoping someone will decide to change things. You have to be willing to confront people lovingly on certain issues. You must be willing to ask questions like, "Why do we do it that way?" This can be a great gift young people bring to a church, because every church needs to re-evaluate.

I am suggesting a couple of factors in the way you question. First, your questions should come, not from simply wanting your own way, but from really caring about the people in that church. If you walk in, and on the first Sunday you want to turn the whole church upside down, people aren't going to think much of it. You may have to wait patiently a few years before people really know that you are committed to them. Your love for people in your church has to be unconditional, not, "If you don't do things my way, I'm leaving."

And also, you have to realize that one man's meat is another man's poison. We all have some basic needs that are the same, but those needs are filled in a lot of different ways. Although a guitar may be best for your kind of singing, if someone else likes hearing Bach, you can't say, "That's junk." A person who's eighteen probably has some different needs from a person who's sixty. When you ask questions and openly listen to the answers, you discover that. There are good reasons for people feeling the way they do, at least part of the time. Developing tolerance and patience with each other is part of what's exciting about the body of Christ.

Frankly, the church is the only institution in our society which has a chance to do this. That's one reason I'm probably more excited about church than anything else in my life today. Every other group is tied to productivity in some way, and those who seemingly can't keep pace and contribute get shunted aside. The old get put in homes. The young aren't listened to. Women get shoved aside. If you can "produce," you're valuable, and your opinions are listened to. Otherwise, forget it.

But the church, the body of Christ, can be different. There's no product involved. Nobody has to be able to work so many hours, put out so much "product." It's one place where the old are valuable, where the young are valuable—just as valuable as anyone else. In the church you can form a community with people truly different from yourself. That's one of the church's most precious gifts. It's the differences in a church that make it valuable. Sameness wouldn't expand your horizons or make you truly grow.

Wrong Question

What good is church? When we ask that question we're usually asking, "What do I get out of it?" And that's the wrong question. There are many benefits that result from our involvement in church. But those benefits can't be realized until we change the question from "What do I get out of it?" to "What am I putting into it?"

The get-what-I-can-get, dog-eat-dog attitude of the world shouldn't exist in the body of Christ. We are to have an attitude of love. Of giving. Of sacrifice. We are governed by the ground rules of the New Testament, the basic rule of which is, "Love your neighbor as yourself." That opens us to genuine security with each other. We discover that when we bare our problems others can help us bear them. There's potential for growth, for support, for friendship, for finding others who will be like an extended family—loving us like surrogate brothers, sisters, aunts, and uncles.

So I'd say this: Allow yourself to be frustrated with church. The only way to avoid frustration is to expect nothing. The church has such great potential and we need to expect a lot. Otherwise we won't reach our potential.

But however frustrated you get, stay with it. Don't cop out by sitting like a mannequin propped up in your pew. Don't stop going. Don't try to run from the differences of opinion you find. Face the problems. And begin to discover the joy that comes with being molded into what God wants you to be. He does it through his body, the church.

TAKEOFF

Be honest. Go ahead and ask yourself the question: "What do I get out of church?" If you're dissatisfied with your answer, compare it to the answer you give this question: "What am I putting into church?"

What are your biggest complaints about church? Do your friends have similar complaints? Individually, or as a group, devise a practical strategy for change based on the modeling concept presented in this chapter.

If you aren't active in a church right now, the best response you could make to this chapter would be to find one you could be a part of.

———○———

The Book of Ephesians contains Paul's analogies of the church as a building and as a body. First Corinthians 12 talks about the diversity in the church. Many of the New Testament letters written to churches provide insights into what the church is expected to be.

Conclusion

WHAT ABOUT ALL THE UNANSWERED QUESTIONS?

D. Michael Hostetler

Sometimes we're afraid God won't be able to survive our doubts and questions.

Conclusion

What About All the Unanswered Questions?

Seeds of doubt are sown throughout our lives. And questions can crop up just about any time. Unfortunately, thousands of Christian kids who have come to know God and are living for him approach these questions with dread. They picture themselves in a biology lecture on evolution, unable to defend their belief in biblical creation. They imagine a psychology teacher who discounts the value of guilt or a religion class in which the professor disagrees with the Bible interpretation of their pastor. Or they imagine themselves talking to a friend who asks a spiritual question they can't answer. And in every one of these imagined scenarios, they feel inadequate to defend or explain what they believe.

That realization can be terrifying. I know because I've talked to many people who have expressed it, and because I've known it myself. I've felt at times that God was depending on my defense of him. I have been afraid my faith wouldn't survive the onslaught of learning and of people who knew so much more about the world than I did.

But as I've grown over the years and as I've talked with other Christians who've hacked their way through the wilds of education, I've begun to relax. I've developed a handful of principles for intellectual survival—principles I can follow confidently as my learning and living raises questions I can't answer.

1. Remember that God and truth are synonymous.

Too many people approach doubts and questions as if they're walking through a hostile wilderness, afraid they're going to kick over a rock and have something jump out and attack God. God is in no danger. We don't have to play great white hunter, protecting God from truth. He *is* truth.

Sometimes we get the impression God's truth and man's truth are totally different. They are only different in quantity; God knows more than we do. But qualitatively they are the same; truth is truth.

Facts are friendly. As Christians we never have to be afraid of truth. Any conflict between "God's truth" and "man's truth" comes from a misunderstanding about one or both of them. They are one and the same.

2. Don't make God say things he doesn't say.

Some of the conflict we see between God's and man's truth results when we attribute more to him than he says. In other words, it's our mistake, not his.

A classic example took place when Galileo proposed the new theory that the planets revolved around the sun. The Christian church insisted that was heresy. From their study of Scripture, the theologians of that day held strong feelings about the centrality of man and the importance of the earth in the universe. Based on those interpretations, they denounced Galileo and insisted Christians had to believe that God placed the sun in orbit around the earth. With their interpretation they made God say something he didn't say.

Eventually the truth became known. But it did not destroy God or Christianity. God wasn't wrong. Man's interpretation of his word was.

There are still differences of interpretation among Christians. Some believe Creation took place in six twenty-four-hour days only a few thousand years ago. Other Christians lean away from the literal twenty-four-hour-day belief.

There's no question of whether or not God could have done it in six days. Of course he could have. The words "can't" and "God" don't rightfully fit in the same sentence. If God *is,* God *can.*

Interpretation also varies on such basic Christian beliefs as the sacraments of baptism, communion, and teaching on the Holy Spirit. Certainly we can hold onto our own interpretations of God's Word; we just need to be careful not to elevate those interpretations to the level of Scripture.

3. Don't make science say things it doesn't.

I've met many Christians who seem terrified of science. Because some scientists are atheists, they feel science itself is anti-God.

True science is basically the business of thinking God's thoughts after him. The scientific method—experimentation, observation, interpretation—is a means of discovering truth.

Christians who fear science are especially edgy about the ability to duplicate some of what God has done. It's as if they're afraid that by creating life in a test tube science will be able to say God didn't create life in the first place. Don't forget that absurd "logic" I used earlier. My father built a house. I watched him build it. Then I built a house. Therefore my father is unnecessary and doesn't exist.

That logic doesn't follow—for building or creating. If anything, mankind's creative ability points to our kinship with a master creator.

We also need to realize that many questions science struggles with (including the theory of evolution) are still open and unsettled, even if some scientists feel otherwise.

4. Learn to hold suspended judgments.

There are a lot of things in the world, in the study of science, even in the study of the Scriptures that we can't understand right now. I've found it helpful to fence off an area of my mind labeled "Suspended Judgments." It's where I put things I don't have enough information to understand.

I can still ask and struggle with the questions when I have the energy or when I receive some new insight. But I don't let the unanswered questions bother me. I know that sometime I'll understand them better. And I can relax instead of worrying about an answer.

5. Avoid a compartmentalized mind.

In an attempt to protect their faith, many people try to divide their living and thinking into two parts—the secular side and the spiritual side. On one hand there is practical truth—how to install a toilet, the psychology of friendship, the social trends of American history. And on the other hand, not to be confused with practical truth, is something theoretical called God's truth—faith, Scripture, spirituality.

It's as if a big saber-toothed tiger of secular truth lives on one side of the mind and we're afraid he's going to massacre the little bunny rabbit of spiritual truth that resides in a small hole on the other side. We try to protect the rabbit by keeping him separate from the tiger. We even categorize schools and subject matter to allow for separate teaching of secular and spiritual truth.

The results can be dangerous. An insistence on an anti-logical, anti-practical, anti-scientific way of thinking about facts is closer to superstition than it is to Christianity. True Christianity touches the world at every level.

Jesus taught that our faith should affect each area of our lives. So we not only disobey his teaching when we segregate our thinking into secular and spiritual levels, but we also lose the chance to strengthen and validate our faith by building it into the whole structure of our lives. That kind of separatist thinking is more of a threat than a defense in the game of intellectual survival.

6. Realize the Bible doesn't tell us everything.

In giving us his truth, God puts restraints on it. For example, when Jesus instructed his disciples to go into all the world and preach the gospel, he didn't give a detailed explanation of geography. He didn't explain that despite popular belief the world was round. He didn't say that one day a guy named Columbus would argue with Queen Isabella and get a boat and sail west until he discovered America. Jesus stuck to his central concern, just as the Bible sticks to central truths. As years passed, that instruction took on new practical meaning for missionaries who learned of other continents. But Jesus' central message remained.

The people of the Old and New Testaments weren't ready for details about orbits, trajectories, or spatial relationships. God limited what he said for the sake of the people of that time. But everything he did say has proven compatible with new knowledge we've gained over the centuries.

We may seem as naive to future generations as people who lived two thousand years ago seem to us today. There are so many things we still don't know about our universe. The numbers of unanswered questions are as infinite as God is. As we learn more answers we'll think of more questions.

If we realize that and get a handle on the principles listed here, we'll be able to face any questions that arise. Learning to live with unanswered questions is part of what it means to be living with God. If we can do it, we'll survive intellectually until the day God gives us complete understanding.

There need be no hurry in our search for all answers. Living with God will be a permanent arrangement.